About the Author

Segun Tewogbola is the president and the senior pastor at Kingdom Truth for All Nations, who was called by God during six months (everyday prayer meeting) at Frances Street, Woolwich, London, United Kingdom. He likes to describe himself as God - addict, preaching the Gospel of the kingdom across the nations of the world. He has written many books, and he speaks in Christian conferences, seminars, and church meetings. He has also preached the kingdom message on radio and television with much passion for the souls. He is happily married to sister, Kehinde.

Speaking Destiny

Segun Tewogbola

Speaking Destiny

Olympia Publishers
London

www.olympiapublishers.com
OLYMPIA PAPERBACK EDITION

Copyright © Segun Tewogbola 2023

The right of Segun Tewogbola to be identified as author of this work has been asserted in accordance with sections 77 and 78 of the Copyright, Designs and Patents Act 1988.

All Rights Reserved

No reproduction, copy or transmission of this publication may be made without written permission.
No paragraph of this publication may be reproduced, copied or transmitted save with the written permission of the publisher, or in accordance with the provisions of the Copyright Act 1956 (as amended).

Any person who commits any unauthorized act in relation to this publication may be liable to criminal prosecution and civil claims for damage.

A CIP catalogue record for this title is available from the British Library.

ISBN: 978-1-80439-280-5

This is a work of fiction.
Names, characters, places and incidents originate from the writer's imagination. Any resemblance to actual persons, living or dead, is purely coincidental.

First Published in 2023

Olympia Publishers
Tallis House
2 Tallis Street
London
EC4Y 0AB

Printed in Great Britain

Dedication

I dedicate this book to the memories of my parents, Pa Francis and Prophetess Dorcas Tewogbola Romimora.

Acknowledgments

Thank you, my sweetheart, Kehinde, for supporting me all the way and all the times!

FOREWORD

I was greatly humbled and challenged when my beloved brother, Segun Tewogbola, asked me to write the foreword to this amazing, timely, and inspirational book called *Speaking Destiny*.

From the introduction to the conclusion, one will be drinking pure Wisdom brewed in the pot of love.

The author's commitment to the Scripture in its right content and context is absolutely worthy of emulation.

In this book, many will come to know that what others call problems are actually challenges and opportunities freely made available to all, especially for every true believer. We are made to understand from this book that destiny is not fully expressed and fulfilled until one reaches his or her assigned destination.

The reader will also discover the place of right planning in life. This will also help both students and humble teachers. Using the experience of Israel on their way to the Promised Land, Segun Tewogbola explained how we can renew and program our minds unto a clear conscience toward God and man, fearlessly and intentionally.

Speaking Destiny, the companion of success, made a bold statement that life begins when you arrive at your destination. One will also gain great insight and lessons from the glorious testimonies and destinies of several great and influential people, from Mother Teresa to Papa Kenneth E. Hagin.

In conclusion, this book, *Speaking Destiny,* is all about the Lord Jesus.

Therefore, without further hesitation, I humbly recommend this book to every true seeker of the Kingdom of God, so as to discover a clear and concise path to fulfilling their destinies to the glory of Christ Jesus through the working of the Indwelling Holy Spirit.

Apostle O Thomas Ojo,
CHRIST TEMPLE INTERNATIONAL, LONDON, U.K.

Introduction

How would you take it, if I should tell you that you have no problem; you are only faced with challenges? You might probably not believe me! Roadblocks, setbacks, and obstacles are forms and types of challenges common to everybody living under the Sun.

A challenge is an instigation intended to convince a person to perform an action he otherwise would not have performed. Challenges provoke us to think a way through the odds facing us in life. Challenges should not be seen as blocking stones, they are indeed stepping stones!

Life is full of challenges, and moreover, because you are a Christian does not mean you will not be faced with challenges. The challenges of my life are not indications that I have not prayed enough. No! Challenges are ways of developing our mental capacity through the tests placed before us in real life.

Apostle Paul faced many challenges in his life and ministry. He wrote some of his challenges thus in one of his epistles:

'I have traveled extensively and have been endangered from rivers, robbers, my own people, and gentiles. I've also been in danger in the city, in the open country, at sea, from false brothers, in toils and hardship, through many a sleepless night, through hunger, thirst, many periods of fasting, coldness, and nakedness.' – **2 Corinthians 11:26/27 (ISV)**

Despite all these challenges, this singular Apostle (Paul) wrote more than half of the books in the New Testament of the Holy Bible!

One would have thought that this man (Paul) had no challenges in life: When he was in prison; he *comforted* the Philippians' Church members that were not in prison, to *rejoice in the Lord always*!

Apostle Paul was a success in ministry by any standard; he was one of the most hardworking Missionaries the world would ever see, and also an erudite teacher and preacher of the gospel of the Kingdom!

This celebrated apostle of our Lord Jesus Christ was not without challenges, but he worked around all his challenges. Hear him again:

'Troubles are around us on every side, but we are not shut in; things are hard for us, but we see a way out of them.' – **2 Corinthians 4:8 (BBE)**

The challenges we are facing in life are not stop signs, but they are actually guide lines to success. Do you also believe that if there is a will, there is a way? Yes, I do believe too.

In a nutshell, what I have been trying to communicate to you is that, until you get to your destination in life, your destiny is not fully expressed, and sometimes it does not make sense to most people around you.

From where you are now, to your destination, which God called His *rest* (for you); there are many challenges which should not stop you from moving on ahead in life. In whatever form or type they appear, you must work a way out of your challenges. Challenges are the Aptitude Test of Life!

For so many years, I hid under religion and blamed

the devils for my inability to work around my challenges in life. It took me time to realize that great thing does not happen by accident, people plan and prepare for it.

My friends, there are various keys that are meant to close and open various doors in life. As important as prayer is as a key, it cannot close door against poverty; the key that does that is hard work! Miracle does not make a man wealthy; it is wisdom that does that - wealth comes not to the fools! So use the right key as you journey along in life, and stop being religious.

Put a lamp on the table top, it fills the room with light. The same experience is recorded for loud speaker; the higher it hangs, the better every one hears it! Your destiny can be better heard and seen from the mountain top than from the valley of life.

Your aspiration is what takes you from the valley to the mountain top in life. Do not wait until you get to the top before you draw your plan.

Your present situation should not affect your dream which is the vehicle of your destiny. If you alter your dream in any way to fit your present situation, you may never arrive at your original, God – given destination.

This is the very reason I have been talking about challenges in life. Work and walk around the challenges of your dream, but do not adulterate your dream! Your dream has a lot to do with your destiny!

Pilate the governor asked Jesus this question, 'are you a king?' Jesus answered him thus:

'For this purpose was I given birth, and for this purpose I came into the world.' – **John 18:37 (BBE)**

To know your purpose in life is to live out your

conviction. Jesus knew His purpose in life, and He lived out His conviction as the King (of kings). Even in the face of a trial which hanged between life and death, Jesus still spelled out His conviction. Today, Jesus is the King of kings and the Lord of lords!

I used to place a postcard in front of my room door at home when I was an undergraduate. It has this quotation which I loved so much then:

'The apparent defeat on the Cross was followed by a tremendous victory of resurrection; I know whom I believe, I am destined to win!'

This speaks volume to me then and even now. I have given my life to Jesus, the One who was, and is, and is to come – surely without an iota of doubt, I am designed and destined to win! It is this conviction that gives me strength as I continue to journey in life.

It is your conviction that will eventually attracts your helpers of destiny, so do not abandon your conviction because of some challenges. Not considering how long, if you will not quit, your destiny will soon be speaking to the whole world about the glory of God!

It is my earnest prayer that you will soon locate the key to success when you focus your conscious mind on things you desire and not on things you fear.

I believe that if one always looked at the skies, one would end up with wings.

You have come to win!
Preparing the Bride,
Segun Tewogbola
April, 2018

Chapter One

What Is Man?

David the King of Israel who God brought from tending his father's sheep to ruling the people of God, was amazed and dazzled on how God brought him from zero to hero, from grass to grace, and from nobody to somebody in life!

At the very peak of his amazement and excitement, King David asked himself this one – million dollar question; what exactly have I done to deserve all these benefits and blessings from God, the Maker of Heaven and Earth? He penned it down in such a way that it involved every mankind - What is man that you would be mindful of him, and the son of man that you care for him? (Psalm 8:4)

The correct answer to the question probing the heart of King David can only be located in the purpose of man on earth. Why God did made man? The wisdom and the purpose of God in creating mankind was the answer the King was looking for.

Before The Beginning!

Our Bible should have introduced God to us from the first Word, from the first sentence, from the first page, from the first book of the Bible. Instead of 'In *the beginning, God created the heaven and the earth.*' –

Genesis 1:1 we should have had it thus: 'God in the beginning created the heaven and the earth.'

The 'beginning' is an indication of time, it is a time factor. But God had been before time began; therefore it is just appropriate to put God first before the element of time (the beginning) at the opening statement of our Bible. The infinite eternity of God could only be made known to us by putting God first before the 'beginning' – which was the beginning of creations, and not the beginning of the Creator!

From the opening account of Genesis, we understand that God first made the heaven, and then the earth. The full account of the creation of heaven was not given to us from this account in Genesis, but we do have a bit detail of the creation of the earth; starting from the earth which was without form and it was void. From this point onward, nothing was said of the heaven from the point of creation.

However, from the book of Revelation in the Bible, there was a record which focused on a war in heaven! Although we might not have full details of how the heaven was created, we learnt there was a war in heaven.

'And there was war in heaven: Michael and his angels fought against the dragon; and the dragon fought and his angels, and prevailed not; neither was their place found any more in heaven. And the great dragon was cast out, that old serpent, called the Devil, and Satan, which deceiveth the whole world: he was cast out into the earth, and his angels were cast out with him.' – **Revelation 12:7 – 9 (KJV)**

Whatever heaven is by definition, there was a war there according to the above verse of the bible. Arch angel Michael and his angels fought violently against the dragon that had rebellion as his reason for waging war against the Authority that had been reigning. Although the dragon and his angels fought, they prevailed not; neither was their place found any more in heaven!

The leader of the rebellion was no other one than the very angel that had once enjoyed many privileges than others – the Devil! The same verse narrowed down the names of the dissident leader to the Devil. He was also the great dragon (*full of fury*), the old serpent (*cunning in nature*), called the devil (*Deceiver*), and Satan (*Accuser*). His primary and main work now is to deceive the whole world.

From the narrative of the war in heaven, there is a significant statement which we need to amplified and looked into accurately; it says, **'neither was their place found any more in heaven.'**

The better translations of the 8th verse of Revelation chapter twelve, have it thus: *'They did not prevail, neither was place found for them (him) any more in heaven.'* The explanation was fully on Devil referred to as him, and not to the fallen angels referred to as them. In other word, the Devil could not find his place any more in heaven.

Howbeit, the bible according to the books of Job and Zachariah, recorded a day when the sons of God came to present themselves before the LORD, and Satan came also among them (Job 1:6 & Zachariah 3: 1- 3)! You might wonder what Satan was doing among the angels since he has lost his place in heaven. The answer is in our understanding of the word 'place' which means 'Position' or 'Office' if you like.

What was the office or position that the Devil held

before he waged war and lost out in heaven? He was a top – notch among the angelic order of Cherub.

There are orders of angels, and we must appreciate the fact that God created them one by one; angels were not mass - produced, and they do not reproduce themselves like mankind. The major orders of angelic beings are the Cherubim and the Seraphim.

Seraphim mean fiery ones, in allusion, as is supposed, to their burning love. They are represented as "standing" above the King as he sat upon his throne, ready at once to minister unto him. Their form appears to have been human, with the addition of wings. This word, in the original, is used elsewhere only of the "fiery serpents" Seraphim are the six – winged angels standing in the Presence of God.

It seems the Seraphim's major purpose of existence is to sing praises to God in God's presence. The 'doorposts and thresholds shook' at the sound of their voices. These are awesome creatures (Isaiah 6:2 – 6)!

Cherubim on the other hand seem to be simple in appearance, with only two set of wings. They are like people with wings. Their primary purpose for existence seems to deliver messages from God to creation, and they are soldiers of the heavenly order.

Satan was of the order of cherubim and his position (his place) was to guard the very throne of God. His position was that of protecting the holiness of God. The function of the cherubim as bearers and movers of the Divine throne is brought out most clearly in the vision of Ezekiel (Ezekiel 1).

Cherubim are represented as four living creatures, each with four faces, man, lion, ox, and eagle; having the figure and hands of men, and the feet of calves. Each has four wings, two of which are stretched upward, meeting above and sustaining the "firmament," that is, the bottom of the Divine throne (Ezekiel 1).

The Garden of Eden

'When they heard the voice of the LORD God as He was walking in the garden during the breeze of the day.' **– Genesis 3:8 (ISV)**

From the verse above, we can simply deduce that the traditional garden of Eden had more than Adam and Eve as its inhabitants. Apparently, if we read between the lines we may reasonable conclude that the Garden of Eden was also the dwelling place of God (Elohim)!

Cherubim bear the throne upon which God descends from His high abode. Thus, in the description of a Theophany in Psalms 18, we read: - *'He bowed the heavens also, and came down; and thick darkness was under his feet. And he rode upon a cherub and did fly; yea, he soared upon the wings of the wind.'* **(Psalms 18:9, 10)** Hence, the Lord of Hosts, is repeatedly styled. *'He that sitteth (throned) above the cherubim.'* **(Psalms 80:1; 99:1 1 Samuel 4:4, etc.).**

'Who maketh the clouds his chariot; Who walketh upon the wings of the wind.' - **Psalms 104:3** - The Hebrew for "chariot" is rekhubh, is a sort of inverted kerubh. So we may deduce that God rides upon the Cherubim to visit or attend the Garden of Eden.

Before the fall of Adam, when he has not eaten of the forbidden fruit, the Garden of Eden was the abode of the gods (elohim). Life was the issue, and light was the substance at the Garden of gods (elohim).

Who exactly was Lucifer?

In our quest to know what man is, that God so much favored him; we need to visit the biblical figure and subject of Lucifer. Surprisingly, this controversial figure was only mentioned once in the bible.

The single place where *Lucifer* is found is in **Isaiah 14:12** it reads;

'How art thou fallen from heaven, O Lucifer, son of the morning!'

The Hebrew word ***Heylel*** which simply means ***shining one*** (Young's Concordance), ***morning star*** (Strong's Exhaustive Concordance), ***bright star or splendid star*** (Gesenius' Hebrew-Chaldee Lexicon), is Lucifer in the Latin word!

While the Hebrew does not indicate this as a personal name, the Latin translators rendered it as such. This is important for us to remember that Lucifer was not a personal name just like Christ is not a personal name but an office.

From the footnote of the Amplified Bible on Isaiah 14:12 you will come across this informative commentary concerning the subject *LUCIFER*:

*'Some students feel that the application of **the name Lucifer to Satan is erroneous,** even though it is commonly taught to that effect. Lucifer,* **THE LIGHT BRINGER,** *is the Latin equivalent of the Greek word phosphorus, which is used as a title of Christ in II Peter 1:19 (... until the DAY STAR arises in your hearts.) and corresponds to the name 'BRIGHT MORNING STAR' in* ***Rev. 22:16****, which Jesus called Himself.* ***The application of*** *the name Lucifer has only existed since the third century A.D., and is based on the* ***supposition*** *that* **Luke 10:18** *(I beheld Satan as lightning fall from heaven) is an*

explanation of Isaiah 14:12, which authorities feel is not true.'

Although the authorities might *feel* this is not true, but there are evidences and facts in addition to the bible (**The 1972 edition of Encyclopedia Britannica (ABB), and The Jewish Encyclopedia)** which back this claim that Satan is not Lucifer:

- There is no reasonable evidence that Isaiah 14 with its popular writing was referring to Satan.

- The Bible calls Satan the ruler of the realm of spiritual darkness, according to Ephesians 6:12 – how can the same Bible refer to Satan as the Light Bearer which is translated Lucifer in Latin? The only other verse we can recall which mentions anything about Satan in reference to light is **II Corinthians 11:14**. It says Satan is able to transform himself into an angel of light, but according to the Greek, the word is not transform -- it is MASQUERADE (Strong's). This is as close as he has ever been to being light -- as a masquerading actor!

- God gave Isaiah the Prophet a parable against the King of Babylon who was an oppressor, and whose death was clearly described in verse 16 of Isaiah 14. Satan is not death yet, so the parable could not have been written for him.

- The subject of the parable, the King of Babylon was called a 'Man' whereas Satan the Accuser of the brethren is a spirit being.

- The man (King) in question is to be buried in shame (Isaiah 14:19, 20)—a circumstance which is not applicable to the devil (see Revelation 20:10).

- A close and careful observation of both the writings of Isaiah 14 and Ezekiel 28 reveals the initial focus of the prophets was on two men who were Kings of Babylon and of Tyre respectively, and not Satan.

- The Holy Spirit would have mentioned and listed the name *'Lucifer'* among the names of Satan He gave to John the beloved in **Revelation 12:9** if truly Satan was Lucifer as we love to believe traditionally.

From the above facts we might conclude that the Lucifer spoken of in **Isaiah 14:12** is not Satan, as some Scholars/authorities also agreed. Now we are closer to the answer King David was searching for which I explained at the beginning of this Chapter.

Reading through the context of Isaiah 14:12, it is obvious that the king of Babylon is the primary concern; but the description given on this verse fits into and reveals Adam as the 'Son of the Morning'!

'How great is your fall from heaven, O shining one, son of the morning! How are you cut down to the earth, low among the dead bodies!' - **Isaiah 14:12 (BBE)**

- God made Adam the exact image and likeliness of God, hence all the attributes of God are expected in Adam (Genesis 1:26).

- Since God is Light and dwells in light according to the Scriptures; 1 John 1:5, James 1:17, 1 Timothy 6:16, etc., therefore, Adam being the son of God (Luke 3:38) is expected to be the shinning one, the son of the morning. And in truth, Adam was clothed in light which was the visible glory of God!

- Since Adam was born of God (Luke 3:38), it was Adam that fell from the Garden (Heaven/Eden/Paradise, see also Ezekiel 28:13); the King of Babylon was already in the fallen state as a man born of a woman.

- It was not Satan who was removed from the

heavens -- **he is still there as of the time Adam fell!** and **Revelation 12:7-11** makes this very clear while **Luke 10:18**(I beheld Satan as lightning falling from heaven) would seem to give credit to the traditional thought; however, if we take it in the context of what had just happened, we will see something else. The falling had actually taken place at the time the seventy were sent by Jesus, when they had cast Satan out of the heavenly dominion he had over the people who were sick and demon possessed. It was at that time He had seen him falling from heaven rather than thousands of years in the past.

- As a result of the fall, God placed a curse upon Adam which says, *'for dust thou art, and unto dust shalt thou return.'* – **Genesis 3:19 (KJV)** This was exactly what Isaiah was referring to when he said, *'how are you cut down to the earth.'* From the writing of Isaiah, this verse (12) was not a question, but an exclamation, because it was happening for the very first time. So the message was not meant for Satan or the King of Babylon, but for Adam.

- **SON OF THE MORNING** gives additional evidence of who this individual might be. In the Hebrew SON (BEN) carries the thought of one who is **B-O-R-N** and is A BUILDER OF A FAMILY NAME. Satan, in his greatest moment, was never born and certainly not given an honorable name from which to build. However, God did bring Adam forth for such a purpose, and for four thousand years he did build the name (nature) that was given to him, even though he had corrupted it. Jesus, the last Adam, then picked up the building tools of the Spirit and finished the work in the glorious realm the first Adam could never do. Yes, indeed, Adam was the **SHINING SON OF THE MORNING** who brought forth the first ray of light to the world. The Lord of Glory then came to finish the work and declared, *'I AM THE BRIGHT AND MORNING STAR.'* - **Revelation 22:16**

- *'Thou hast been in Eden, the Garden of God'* - ***Ezekiel 28:13*** In a letter from Bill Britton to a pastor, he wrote "As for Satan being 'Lucifer' (King James Version only) of Isaiah 14 and Ezekiel 28, consider this... this being who fell was described as holy and beautiful and wise before he fell, and was described as being in the Garden of God, walking among the stones of fire, etc. Read Genesis account of creation, and find that the Garden was prepared for ADAM, not Satan, and that according to the 'gap theory' (a foundation for the Holy Angel Lucifer theory), the Garden was not even created until after 'Lucifer' was supposed to have fallen and become Satan. So, Satan could not have walked in the Garden of God in a holy state."

'MAN, is the one who has been all the things **Isaiah 14 and Ezekiel 28** speak of; namely, LUCIFER, the resident of EDEN, the BEAUTIFUL ONE, the PRINCE OF GOD, even the SHINING CHERUB among the STONES OF FIRE. He was in Eden, the Garden of God, in Paradise, in Heaven, ruling from the Mountain of God and among the Stones of fire -- radiating the glory of his creator.' – Elwin R. Roach

All the explanations above were to provide answers to the question King David asked, and the quote from Elwin Roach (above) would have been a pleasing answer to the King's heart.

In agreement to all of the above, King David further

wrote the wonder of God in placing man above the works of His hands:

'When I look at your skies that your fingers made: I see the moon, I see the stars, You gave them all a place. Then I asked: why do you remember men (and women)? You made their place a little below God. You made them feel as Kings. You made them to rule everything that your hands made. You put everything under their feet: sheep and cows, wild animals in the fields, birds in the air, fish in the waters, monsters in the deep seas. LORD, You are our most powerful King. Your Name is famous in all the wide world.' –**Psalm 8:3 - 9 (Easy English)**

It is therefore necessary for every man and woman of destiny to fully understand how God sees him or her – as Man! God has made man to rule everything His hands had made. Man is elohim.

It is this inner conviction of who you are which births the confidence that overcomes every challenges of life facing you as man. You are wired and prepared by God to win in life. The nature, the time and the seasons are arranged to favor your course in life.

Better still, the scepter of Kingship which Adam dropped due to his gross disobedience and untold rebellious toward God, was picked up again by total obedience and unequal submission of Jesus Christ to God's will, is now being handed over those that gave their lives to Jesus!

The purpose of man in creation is to be in fellowship and to worship God his Maker continuously. This is the reason God adorned man so much with glory and honor. It was because of King Ahasuerus that queen Vashti was adorned with so much pageantry. In the same manner, man was made (glorious) to appear before God in fellowship and in worship – glorious!

After creating Adam, God did not give the first man any religion, but a job with a duty to perform. However, on a daily basis, God desired his fellowship and worship. In whatever area is your calling or passion, you must remember that the ultimate of your living is to fellowship with God and to worship the King of kings.

Ever before King David was born, the patriarch Job had asked this same question that was later tagged to David the King of Israel; what is man? Job penned it down like this:

'What is man, that you have made him great, and that your attention is fixed on him, and that your hand is on him every morning, and that you are testing him every minute?' – **Job 7:17 – 18 (BBE)**

Bible, the book of books finally came out with a reasonable conclusion to this question of life which has been on man's mind from ages past.

The Bible through King Solomon provided the answer in simple and understandable summary thus:

'Let the conclusion of all these thoughts be heard: Fear God and obey his commandments, for this is what it means to be human.' – **Ecclesiastes 12:13 (ISV)**

Chapter Two

Don't Excuse Success Out

You will need to be thoroughly schooled in the things of the Spirit, so that you may understand and identify the sure difference between coincidence and providence. Many other things in life may look alike to an untrained mind, but may not necessarily be the same naturally.

From the simple dictionary definition; coincidence is the property of being coincident; occurring at the same time or place. Providence on the other hand is the manifestation of divine care or direction; an instance of divine intervention. It is a careful governance and guidance of God (or other deity, nature, etc.).

As you journey along your path of destiny, God may be talking to you through nature and other means possible. Providence at this time should be identified and separated from mere coincidence. Coincidence might be a part of probability theory, but providence is definitely not.

Never lose your appetite on God's provision. The Israelites lost their appetite on Manna, the provision from God for His Children in the wilderness. Israel confused providence with coincidence and they lost out on the long run, with their elders dead in the wilderness.

Remember that Israel left Egypt with their cattle or

sheep if you like (Exodus 10:26), so why were they craving and crying for meat when they have these animals with them? In the first instance, unlike cattle, Manna does not require an intense preparation before eating it. As of this time Israel was on a mission (to the Promised Land), not in an occasion to celebrate – they must keep moving on. Secondly, they have not yet renewed their mind – from slaves to a free nation! So the people demonstrated in the wilderness against Moses, the servant of God.

When Israel crossed the Red Sea, God changed their status (no more slaves), but their slavery mentality remained with them until they crossed Jordan. When God changes your status, you must change your nature by renewing your mind. Many destinies have crossed the Red Sea, but they are yet to cross Jordan where they die to self.

'Do not let yourselves be like the people who belong to this world. But instead, let God change how you think. Then you will become new people. You will be able to understand what God wants you to do. You will understand what is good. You will understand what makes God happy. And you will understand how to live completely as God wants you to live.' – **Romans 12:2 (Easy English).**

After four hundred and thirty years of slavery, on their way to the Promised Land, the Children of Israel were not thinking in their minds of how God set them free, but they were thinking of how God has 'failed' them in not providing them with meat in the wilderness – they were sad, and regret being freed from slavery. Pathetic minds!

Until you understand the mind of mankind, you may not know why the Israelite soon forgot the joy of their liberation from slavery, and lament on the absence of meat while on their way to the Promised Land.

Man is made up of hundreds of emotions located tightly in the invisible part of the body: The *long - lasting* emotions like hate, anger, fears, shame, guilt, gloom, blame, grief, etc. And some *short - lasting* emotions too like joy, ecstasy, elation, laughter, love, etc. This explains why we remember what we ought to forget, and forget what we ought to remember? Our minds need a kind of re – programming in order to attain a successful nature which makes it easier for us to fulfill our destinies in life.

Let God Change How You Think!

It may interest you that we are **Beings** first, and **Humans** latter. Although we are called human beings; the physical human part is in minority of just about one percent of the total body, while the Invisible part, the being portion is about ninety nine percent the total body.

Man was made a tripartite creature with a spirit which has a soul that lives in a body. The spirit part of Adam was the breath of the Almighty God, while his soul which is called the mind contains his *will*, his *emotions* and his *intellect*, and finally his physical and physiological body.

Although the bible used the mind and the heart interchangeably, but we know that your heart is located around your chest, and your mind is at your forehead. The brain is the physical anatomy located at your forehead, and the mind is what the brain generates through its activity.

The soul of a man is his mind which is believed to be a powerful part of the being of every human. It is in the mind that decisions which affect life are made; only to be carried out by the body.

The mind is divided into three levels namely:
- **Conscious Mind**: This defines and includes all thoughts and actions within our awareness.
- **Subconscious Mind**: This area of the mind defines all reactions and automatic actions we can become aware of if we think about them.
- **Unconscious Mind**: All past events and memories inaccessible to us no matter how hard we try to remember so as to bring them up.

According to Genesis 2:21 – 23, God caused a deep sleep to fall upon Adam (*Unconscious*), the very moment Adam saw Eve, he said (*Subconscious*), this is a bone of my bones and flesh of my flesh. Thereafter, Adam (*Conscious*) took Eve to himself.

The subconscious mind is the storage room of everything that is currently not in our conscious mind. It stores and retrieves data from all of our past life experiences, our beliefs, our skills, our memories, our past situations, and all images and pictures we have ever seen. It is beneath the conscious mind.

The subconscious mind has the capacity that is far beyond what we think it has. Our thought – pattern defines our lives, and our subconscious mind controls our thought – pattern. It regulates most of our actions and in charge of our learned behavior.

The subconscious mind is referred to in the bible as

the *heart and its thought* (Psalm 139 23 – 24), as the *stronghold* (2 Corinthians 10:3 – 6), as *deceitful and desperately wicked* (Jeremiah 17:9), as *inward and hidden part* (Psalm 51:6), etc. **Cheder** is the Hebrew word for innermost part or the hidden chamber. Of the 38 Scriptures that used cheder, over half of those verses refer to a *secret* (Proverbs 20:27 for example).

Thoughts and feelings in our life that are not scriptural, and we do not deal with immediately and open up to God, are automatically rolled down to the subconscious mind, and eventually become a hidden secret. All our fears, immoralities, insecurities, doubt, etc. That we secretly pushed down to the subconscious mind, thinking no one will know, can invariably control and direct our lives!

One of the most critical variables in stimulating change, the renewing of our minds is overcoming the *silent negativity* of the mind. The mind quietly produces about forty thousand to fifty thousand thoughts per day of which only about ten percent is perceived by the average person. More so, about eighty percent of all hidden thoughts are negative which is basis for people's fear and failure.

For the Christian, the Word of God is the answer to renewing their (subconscious) minds to a desired outcome according to God's higher intelligence of creation (Romans 12:2). The scientific term for this is called **Neuroplasticity**, which is the change in the neural pathways and synapses that occurs due to certain factors like behaviors, environment, or neural processes. During such changes, the brain engages in synaptic pruning, deleting the neural connections that are no longer necessary or useful, and strengthening the necessary ones.

The struggle is that many Christians don't give the Word of God enough time and attention, with the right understanding, to effect the necessary changes which are the renewing in their minds to see lasting results.

Your thoughts are the mainframe and the pillars upon which your actions are seated. Success or failure is a reflection of your action; God is not partial when it comes to obedience. Jesus Christ **walked and worked** on the platform of positive thinking which emanates from His mind. The Bible so advised Christian to attain the mind of Christ (Philippians 2:5). Your mind plays an important role when it comes to success.

'For as he thinks within himself, so he is.' - **Proverbs 23:7 (ISV).**

The starting point with humans is *thoughts*, then feelings, then emotions, and attitudes later. Events in real life trigger off basic *thoughts* of fears and doubts, love and confidence, etc., which evolve later into feelings. These feelings can be positive or negative.

In the process of time, *feelings* are experienced as emotions of light or heavy, joy or hate. Next, these *emotions* in time affect our reactions and shape – up our behavior. Behavior can be constructive or destructive. Our *behaviors* lead to moods which become our *attitudes* as time progresses.

Attitudes which are the most important trait in success can be good or bad. When we refuse to change ourselves for better, we are undoing ourselves; this is our **destiny** in the making, and we are the architects. We are the creators of our destinies; starting with thoughts which gradually progress to feelings, emotions, behaviors, moods, and finally attitudes! We then wrongfully put the blame on God for deciding our destiny, and seek remedies from mere religion.

A sound mind is what God gave us at creation, and this is how we all appeared at birth – with a sound mind! However, the external environment has a lot of influence on a child as he grows in life. Although the parents advice, the child learnt from their lifestyles. Soon the mind of the child is distorted. To make the right choice becomes an issue for the child as he grows.

'For God hath not given us the spirit of fear; but of power, and of love, and of a sound mind.' – **2 Timothy 1:7 (KJV)**

Except we renew our minds to love people and use things, we might end up to use people and love things. A sound mind is a balanced mind that sees good in everything. The spirit of fear cannot operate in a sound mind.

To get rid of fear which might impair your sense of judgment, you will need these three:
- Spirit of Power – with the ability to influence or control.
- Spirit of Love – with the feeling of trust and security.
- Sound Mind – with the balanced perspective to life.

When the spirit of fear engages a man, he ends up suspecting everybody and everything. It is so bad that such a man may not identify or recognize opportunity when it comes knocking at his door.

Many people have excused success out from their lives because of doubt and fear coming from their minds. To be Anxiety-Free is to gain freedom from fears and project strength from within your mind. God did not promised us that things would not be difficult, but He sure promised us that with Him, nothing shall be impossible!

Limits exist only in the mind! Once you can deal with the issues of mind, you are on your way to success.

The way to success may be long and rough, but it is still the way to success. Since limit exists in the mind, the key that unlocks it – Determination is also of the mind! If you could not go far in your mind, you cannot go far in life. This is how God put it across to Abraham:

'I will give you all the land that you can see. I will give it to you and your descendants for all time.' – **Genesis 13:15 (Easy English)**

It was so certain that if Abraham could not see the land, God would not give the land to Abraham. On the natural clime, if Abraham should have problem with his eyes, say short – sightedness for example, he would not have seen far. On the other hand, if Abraham should have problem with his mind, he would not have seen far also in every sense of seeing.

Abraham's descendants got to the edge of the land that Abraham saw, but they were not able to possess the land which God had promised their father, because of the limits in their mind. Hear what the Bible says:

'We also saw the people called Nephilim there. (The descendants of Anak are also Nephilim.) 'And we felt like very small insects when we looked at them. And we seemed like very small insects to them too.' – **Numbers 13:33 (Easy English)**

The descendants of Abraham who were to possess the land God promised Abraham could not do so because of how they *felt* within themselves – *very small insects!* I have stated it earlier that your thoughts are the pillars of your destiny. Control your thoughts and you will soon be giving direction to your life.

On getting to the land God Almighty promised their father Abraham, these children of faith could not aligned their thoughts to the eternal word of God that can never fail. Soon, their *thoughts* became their *feelings* (they felt like very small insects), and their feelings grew to their *emotion* (defeated), which in turn became their *reaction* also known as *behavior* (they withdrew), and later became their *attitude* (incompetence).

Except for Caleb and Joshua that did not share in their thoughts, the land would have remained with the Anakites, and the promise of God would have been unfulfilled (God forbid) to that generation.

Let it be known to you that all the promises of God (to you) are in the custodian of the giants (challenges and limits). You will need to rise up, concentrate and be focused, be determined, and possess your possessions. Life itself is stingy.

In most cases, limits are psychological restrictions placed on the path of success, so as to make you quit the journey and turn back home. While challenges are mostly external, limits are of the mind. It takes a man with dogged determination to overcome both challenges and limits set on his path of destiny.

All the natural resources of this world are hidden deep in the earth.

Nothing good comes easy.

Chapter Three

The Three Ways

In this present world which we called the jet age, things are moving so fast, and these populations under the Sun are not so much keen about how you get what you have, but what matters to them is result. They bluntly refused and disagreed that a man's life does not consist of what he has. This generation has thrown caution to the wind so as to gather possessions. These children have formed a long queue behind *what you have*, and have deserted the line of *who you are*.

The Corporate organizations of the world are so much passionate about money that they only engage in cosmetic sympathy and esoteric projects in their communities. Free and fair elections are fast becoming a thing of the past in world that is thirsty of power. Religious bodies and their affiliates are no more thinking of heaven, but are fast erecting their kingdoms here on earth. The constitution and the composition of Marriage institution are rapidly changing with this fast changing world where baby mama may not necessarily be the wife in the home.

The rat race has started for quite a long time now, and there are neither lanes, tracks nor rules governing the race. We are now in a period similar to the time Israel was without a king; and every man did that which was right in his own eyes (Judges 17:6).

From creation, God attained success for His works with the remarks from the Bible which says, *'Now God saw all that He had made, and indeed, it was very good,'* – **Genesis 1:31 (ISV).** *'Very good'* is another word for excellent! How would God attain this excellent re (mark) if we do not have the account of the creations? God looked at all His works and He was pleased with it – because they were all done in the right manner and method. God was not just looking at the results, but also how He got the results.

In the light of this, God told Joshua about *'Good Success'* which contains both the methodology and the results. God spoke thus:

'For then thou shalt make thy way prosperous, and then thou shalt have good success.' – **Joshua 1:8 (KJV)**

From the above verse, we can reasonably say that if there is good success, there must be bad success. A success is good because of the ways and manners it was accomplished. On the same platform, a success is bad because of the ways and manners it was accomplished.

A hired assassin that drives expensive cars about town, and dresses gorgeously may be successful according to world's standard which looks only into results, but as far as God is concerned, he is not a *'good success'* simply because his ways are not prosperous. The man in question cannot come out openly and tell people what he is doing as business.

Prosperity must always go ahead of any good success; it is the clean and clear methodology engaged to accomplish a good success. Day by day, the bible gave us the detailed account of creations – there was prosperity in the creations, and so there was good success. The big – bang theory of creation was magical on hearing, with no prosperity in its contents.

In summary we can then say that a success is defined by the way it is accomplished. This way (*manner, belief or faith*) is what was recorded in the book of Acts of the Apostle, which was not meant to be road or path:

'Now about that time a great commotion broke out concerning the Way.' – **Acts 19:23 (ISV)**

The above Scripture was actually referring to Christian Faith as a way of life when it mentioned 'the Way' (see also **Acts 9:2, 19:9, 24:22**).

This same way of living is what Jesus meant when He said:

'I am the way, the truth, and the life: no man cometh unto the Father, but by me.' – **John 14:6 (KJV)**

The way is the manners of living out the teaching of Jesus Christ which is based on the gospel of the Kingdom. Jesus once told the Jews that believed in Him to continue in His word; that is to live out the teachings of the Kingdom which He taught them.

Once we have established that the 'Way' in the context of the bible does not refer in any how to paths or roads which we walk, but the manners of doing thing, a belief and/or faith, then we can observe and examine how people arrived at their success.

There are three major ways that people engaged upon to accomplish their desired goals and objectives in life. These major ways have a lot to do about our destinies in life. It is therefore important for us to open up and examine these ways so that we might take to correction and be encouraged in our pursuit of success which propels us to reach our destiny with ease.

- **The Broad Way**: As the name suggest, more than seventy five percent of the people with eagerness for success go this way. It is the way of the gentile where the priests (Pastors) eat the sins of the people.

'For wide is the gate, and broad is the way, that leadeth to destruction, and many there be which go in there at.' – **Matthew 7:13 (KJV)**

Breaking this statement of Jesus Christ down to smaller units with interpretation, we would have the broad way pictured like this:

a) The gate which is the point of entrance is wide which means coming through this gate is a piece of cake. This gate is easily entered. Therefore it can have a lot of traffic passing through this wide gate all at the same time.

b) The way itself is broad; meaning that it is easily trodden. No discipline is required to travel on the broad way.

c) Although a higher percentage of people travel through this way, yet it leads to destruction.

d) Despite the destruction that terminates this way; many people are lured to travel through this way in life.

On the broad way, *smartness* is exalted more than wisdom, and sin is not a reproach. Here, the people that travel on this way are closer to their religious leaders than to God. It is very hard for this group of people to believe that anointing is not in numbers; the more their numbers, the more their false confidence increases, the more they are deceived! These set of people do not always have a permanent testimony. Jesus said that the end of this way is destruction; therefore the pilgrims on this way always end it up with regrets. It is better to ignore the bait than to struggle in the snare. This is the caution attached to life on the broad way.

God spoke extensively about this way to Ezekiel the prophet. In His charge against Israel; God accused some priests for encouraging the people to go astray (the broad way) – away from the ordinances of God. Hear Him:

'And the Levites that are gone away far from me, when Israel went astray, which went astray away from me after their idols; they shall even bear their iniquity. Yet they shall be ministers in my sanctuary, having charge at the gates of the house, and ministering to the house: they shall slay the burnt offering and the sacrifice for the people, and they shall stand before them to minister unto them. Because they ministered unto them before their idols, and caused the house of Israel to fall into iniquity; therefore have I lifted up mine hand against them, saith the Lord GOD, and they shall bear their iniquity. And they shall not come near unto me, to do the office of a priest unto me, nor to come near to any of my holy things, in the most holy place: but they shall bear their shame, and their abominations which they have committed.' – **Ezekiel 44:10 – 13 (KJV)**

There are some key words that God used when speaking with Ezekiel from the above Scripture; those words gave us the vivid pictures of the broad way. The broad way is the rebellious way! Israel went away from God, and worse still some Levites (Pastors) went with Israel, instead of these Priests to bring Israel back to God.

God accused these Levites (Pastors) of **gone away** because it was a deliberate and intentional decision. God however accused Israel of **went astray** because they were not skilled in the ways of the Lord God. Eventually, both the Levites, and Israel became rebellious.

Israel, according to God, ***went after their idols***. They had a choice between God and their idols (evil and perverse ways), but they chose their idols. So, those journeying on the broad way had a choice at hand. The reason we hear so many perverse and dishonoring testimonies coming from those traveling on the broad way. ***They shall bear their iniquity*** – God will put the sins of Israel (Congregation) who went after idols, upon the heads of the Levites (Pastors) who refused to correct their congregation and bring them back to God.

Ministers in my sanctuary - Interestingly, those Levites (Pastors) shall continue to bear their titles and offices. Another important picture from the charge against the Levites (Pastors) is ***having charge at the gates of the house*** (Church) – this is very deep in interpretation and application! The gates at the house (Church) are the Outer Court where newly convinced and converted souls are just coming through, in order to know God better. These gates are always with the highest numbers of believers (Mega), and the Levites (Pastors) that have gone away from God are allowed to have charge of these Congregations at the gates!

From the time of Aaron as the High Priest up until now, God has been calling the Levites (Pastors) to minister unto Him.

'And take thou Aaron thy brother, and his sons with him, from among the children of Israel, that he may MINISTER UNTO ME in the priest's office, even Aaron, Nadab and Abihu, Eleazer and Ithamar, Aaron's sons.' - **Exodus 28:1 (KJV)**(Emphasis mine).

However, since the incidence of Israel's and the Levites (Pastors) abandoning God by choice, He also has abandoned these Levites (Pastors) to shepherd the strayed Israel (Congregation) - ***they shall stand before them to minister unto them*** – so instead of these Pastors (Levites) with titles and accolades to stand before God and minister to God, they are busy ministering to the needs of the congregations (Israel) who had deliberately chosen to do perverse wickedness on a daily basis. Instead of these Pastors (Levites) to serve God, they love to be served as they eat and show off the wealth of the gentiles! Hmnn!

Jeremiah had a similar experience with what some of us are seeing today in these rebellious pastors that parade themselves around the world as the Messiah incarnate; exploiting their congregation's foolishness. Just a minute, read this:

'Then I said, 'these are only poor, they are foolish, for they don't know the LORD's way, the requirement of their God. The prophets prophesy falsely, the priests rule by their own authority, and my people love it this way. But what will you do in the end?' – **Jeremiah 5:4, 31 (ISV)**.

On a final note, the people on the broad way shall continually experience scandals which God called *shame*, when He was speaking to Ezekiel the prophet. From the parallel Scripture, Jesus spoke a hard truth to His disciples, and the bible says, *'From that time many of his disciples went back, and walked no more with him.'* – **John 6:66** (a 666 Scripture – just joking!). The people on the broad way cannot walk in the truth, no matter their religiosity.

- **The Narrow Way**: In its simplest form this way is only speaking about a discipline life. When a focus life is coupled with discipline, the result is always successful.

'How narrow is the gate, and restricted is the way that leads to life! Few are those who find it.' – **Matthew 7:14 (WEB)**

From the verse above, we can easily open up the followings:

a) The entry point which is the gate is narrow; you have to decide and determine first before approaching this gate.

b) The way is restricted; it does not allow any type of indiscipline. You cannot do as you like – it is not all about pleasure, it is about principle.

c) This way invariable leads to life. Life is light, light is knowledge, knowledge is power.

d) Only few (about twenty five percent) who can run their race with patience find this gate.

One important thing we must take home is that the narrow way does not imply one being poor; it is all about doing things right in all strict sense. Above all, the narrow way is used to symbolize the discipline we all need to make it to heaven.

Where there is no vision, the people lose constraint – meaning the people can do anyhow, nothing stops them. This is one of the characteristics of the broad way. However, on the narrow way, there is vision, and the people are constrained.

Jesus the Son of God took the narrow way:

'And though he was a Son, through the pain which he underwent, the knowledge came to him of what it was to be under God's orders.' – **Hebrews 5:8 (BBE)**

Patience is one of the virtues to be learnt on the narrow way. Those traveling on this way need to do directly or indirectly with patience. The narrow way is the way of faith in God, which has to do with patience.

This patience is to be expressed in three major directions:

1. Patience with God: God will do what He has promised you in His own chosen time – you cannot hurry Him up in any way, so be patient with God.

2. Patience with people: Do not fret and take it out on people around you because you are yet to receive your promise. Do not be touchy in anyhow.

3. Patience with yourself: Do not take it out upon yourself, you are not the cause – you only need to be patience because of the way you chose.

'We do not want you to become lazy. You must copy the example of those people who continue believing God. They go on being very patient. And so, they receive what God has promised.' - **Hebrews 6:12 (Easy English).**

If God sends you on a stony path, He will provide boots for you. This is true for the pilgrims on the narrow way of destiny; there is always sufficient grace for them!

While the broad way is encouraging possessions, the narrow way is encouraging characters. *What you have* is a matter of concern on the broad way, but *who you are* is the concern on the narrow way. The reason those with bags and baggage of vanity cannot travel and pass through the narrow way.

- **The Highway:** In a sense, this is the way that God chose to compensate those pilgrims who have endured discipline and chastisement (tutelage of God) while journeying on the narrow way. In actual fact, the narrow way eventually leads to the high way in life.

'And a highway will be there; its name will be, The Holy Way; the unclean and the sinner may not go over it, and those who go on it will not be turned out of the way by the foolish.' – **Isaiah 35:8 (BBE)**

When it comes to applications, the above verse is important for those believers who have chosen to live a righteous life by the grace of God. The following observations were derived from the verse:

a) The Hebrew word **caalal** which means to **cast up** gave us the picture of road construction (especially for armies) whereby valleys were filled up, hills, obstacles, and obstructions were removed and so we have the highway (express way)! This is the starting point where the pilgrims receive divine encouragements to continue in righteousness (Righteousness exalts a nation).

b) The way is called The Holy Way, because it is God Who profits His servants. It should be noted that all those conscious righteousness of the pilgrims, after a while, are now becoming unconscious holiness. God is using these victors to tell the world that holiness profits. It is the way God Himself guides and leads His people!

c) The unclean and sinner will now see the profit and the gain of waiting upon the Lord God. However, they cannot cross lane now, except they go all the way back and start all over on the narrow way.

d) Even fools – the simples, will not go astray because God shall be with them on this high way!

In general, Apostle Peter put the journey from the narrow way to the highway in words like this:

'But the God of all grace, who hath called us unto his eternal glory by Christ Jesus, after that ye have suffered a while, make you perfect, stablish, strengthen, settle you.' – **1 Peter 5:10 (KJV)**

The word, Character was from the word Chisel – meaning that God chisel out our character with His disciplines which the above verse recorded as *suffered a while*. What happens after this while should be of interest to all *passing through* the narrow way:

1. God makes you **perfect** – tested and trusted life.
2. God **establish** you – lay a solid foundation for your destiny.
3. God **strengthen**s you – God brings you helpers who are experts!
4. God **settles** you – This is restoration on every area of your life!

All what the hasty and impatient pilgrims were trying to *get* on the Broadway, God will now *give* to you freely on the highway.

The highway is characterized by the presence of few people which also depicts the picture of the mountain top. At the highway, you can have peace of mind because of the absence of unnecessary pressure. The Psalmist observed life on the highway and penned his experience down like this: *'You will make clear to me the way of life; where you are joy is complete; in your right hand there are pleasures forever and ever.'* – **Psalm 16:11**

At the end of the day, we will realize that God is happy when His people prosper and succeed according to His plan and purpose. The Psalmist put it simply that God has pleasure in the prosperity of His servants – Psalm 35:27!

The survivors of the narrow way, who refused to compromised but determined to the highway, are engrossed with the issue of holiness, and how to please God daily, despite the prosperities that God has bestowed upon their lives.

Abraham was already rich before God called him to the highway of life! This man, Abraham had about 318 men in his household which fed daily with food! After he proved his allegiance and loyalty to God through the (attempted) sacrifice of his son, Isaac – God then promised (the rich) Abraham blessings! It was recorded thus in the bible:

'I will indeed bless you, and I will greatly multiply your descendants…' – **Genesis 22:17 (NET)**

The word to examine carefully from the promise of God to Abraham is INDEED – I will *indeed bless* you!

This was the same ultimate blessing that Jabez was asking God for in his prayer – which is very popular today.

'And Jabez called on the God of Israel, saying, Oh that thou wouldest bless me indeed,' - **1 Chronicles 4:10 (KJV)**

The indeed blessing is the proof of God's attestation to those who made it to the highway (of holiness) of life. It also makes sense that God will not give big assignment to men of small character; it will end up in crisis, whereby the name of the LORD God is profaned. Hence, the highway blessing is *indeed blessing* reserved for those who have passed through the narrow way!

Considering the classical interpretations of these three ways; we will find out that the Broadway leads to destruction, probably the lake of fire which is popularly called hell.

The narrow way is always the discipline way of life that does not encourage sins, and every form of evil and wickedness. Here people endure and persevere discipline while they continue their journey to heaven of God. Character is formed here on the narrow way.

The highway is the ultimate of the three ways; it is tagged the way of holiness. God has made expressway out from the narrow way – the blessing and the joy of heaven begins with the recipients here on the highway

Acting wisely is the way of life - Proverbs 15:24

Chapter Four

When Manna Ceased

It was G. Macdonald that said; to have what we want is riches, but to be able to do without it is power.

God's intention is to raise a strong set of children that can occupy the land for Him. So in God's wisdom, He placed power over and above riches. Although both are given to God's children at the *appointed time*. It has always being God's satisfaction to train and raise His Children in the *process of time* until they are powerful enough, and then He ushers them through the *fullness of time* into abundant riches.

When we were in the High School, there was an internal examination for all the final year students which was called the Mock Examinations. This examination was to prepare the final year students for the External examinations. In most cases, and in many schools, this mock examination was always tougher than the real final external examinations.

All what you need to breakthrough in life are not as tough as what you have acquired when you were passing through in life. The life's Mock Examinations are always tougher than life Promotion Examinations.

When Israel left Egypt, God started feeding them with Manna for good forty years! The same food every day! Soon, Israel lost their appetite from God's provision - they cried out for meat; they long for Egypt, the place of their slavery.

Why would a loving God put His Children to such trial? The answer to this question is found in the Bible thus:

'Who fed thee in the wilderness with manna, which thy fathers knew not, that he might humble thee, and that he might prove thee, to do thee good at thy latter end.' - **Deuteronomy 8:16(KJV)**

Another bible translation put it this way:

'He fed you with manna in the wilderness, a food unknown to your ancestors. He did this to humble you and test you for your own good.' - **Deuteronomy 8:16 (NLT)**

From this Scripture, we can deduce the followings:

1. God fed Israel with Manna in the wilderness (a place of transition).

2. God fed Israel with Manna, so as to humble them.

3. The feed (Manna) was to test the Children of God.

4. God used Manna to prepare Israel to live well in the days to come - it was for their own good!

At the inception of Manna, Israel took it with levity; asking the question, what is this? Before long, these people in transit abused the grace of provision by asking Moses for meat. The children of Jacob craved for the delicacy of slavery.

The abundance supply of quail to the Israelite was not a miracle in the long run; it was a kind of scolding for a child who would not trust his father.

This is how the Bible put it:

'And the people stood up all that day, and all that

night, and all the next day, and they gathered the quails: he that gathered least gathered ten homers: and they spread them all abroad for themselves round about the camp. And while the flesh was yet between their teeth, ere it was chewed, the wrath of the LORD was kindled against the people, and the LORD smote the people with a very great plague.' - **Numbers 11:32 - 33 (KJV)**

At the end of it all, Israel learned their lesson; not to murmur against God's provisions. Manna became Israel's regular daily diet which they await its supply morning by morning in the wilderness. God has forcefully closed the door of murmuring, and the door of thanksgiving was left open for whosoever cares.

It is good for us to examine or give a good analysis of what Manna actually looked like in those days.

1. It was like flakes - very thin in thickness.
2. It has almost a similar taste of Coriander.
3. It can melt under intense heat.
4. It has to be picked up in large quantity.
5. Its supply came directly from Heaven.
6. It cannot be stored up for later days.
7. It has no health hazard.

The nature of Manna as food to be taken (three times a day) daily would naturally requires the body to drink water a lot. With about three and half million people traveling in the wilderness, after eating Manna, how did they get water to drink daily, bearing in mind that an average person will consume about 5 gallons of water per day?

With the divine supply of Manna comes the provision of water for the people of God right in the wilderness and deserts! The supply of water for forty years through the wilderness was a miracle on its own. People may do without food for some days, but not so with water. Water is life!

Who will counsel God?

God in His wisdom knew the extreme temperatures of the deserts, and He made divine provisions for the two extreme temperatures as His Children were traveling through the desert.

The Deserts are extremely hot in the day time, and are extremely cold in the night time. Those who have been to the mountain will understand fairly these extreme temperature differences. So, God provided for Israel, the Pillar of Cloud in the day, to blanket and cushion the heat from the excessive temperature of the day. In the same manner, God provided the Pillar of Fire for Israel, to supply flame necessary to heat up the Camp at night, so as to heat up the extreme cold temperature at night.

God did all the miracles for Israel while passing the wilderness, about to arrive and entered into the Promised Land. The conditions were not appreciated by the Children of Israel despite the miraculous signs and wonders it entails. So they continued their journey with many trials, temptations, and challenges on the way, but the manner was a constant factor - a reminder of God's faithfulness on the journey.

Although they were no more slaves, the Children of Israel accepted their fate of transiting from one settlement to another with the regular supply of Manna from heaven. These Children of promise envied other nations, and pray to be like the nations they met on their way to the Promised Land.

Until when you arrive at your destination, everything

you do will be temporary in life. The closer they were to the Promised Land, the more frustrated they were - but they have learned never to murmur on God's provision again.

Gilgal: The place called Gilgal has a significant position in the journey of Israel, from Egypt to the Promised Land. It is also important for us today to have a close look at Gilgal as we study Israel on our way to the Promised Land - Heaven.

Elisha followed Elijah to Gilgal, before he received the mantle of leadership from his master, Elijah. Israel passed through Gilgal before entering the Promised Land. Is Gilgal not relevantly important for all of us before we could inherit the Promises?

'And this is the cause why Joshua did circumcise: All the people that came out of Egypt, that were males, even all the men of war, died in the wilderness by the way, after they came out of Egypt.' - **Joshua 5:4 (KJV)**

At Gilgal, we all must put away the foreskin of our body(Circumcision) which is the putting away of the Self. Apostle Paul expound on this subject when he wrote the Philippians thus:

'For we are the circumcision, which worship God in the Spirit, and rejoice in Christ Jesus, and have no confidence in the flesh.'
- Philippians 3:3 (KJV)

It is important not to allow flesh to survive and live beyond Gilgal. The flesh must be done away with and subdued and subjected to the ruling of the Spirit. God does not bless the carnal man, otherwise it ends in Crisis.

God commanded Joshua to carry out this circumcision, the second of its kind, after all the men of war had died in the wilderness. These men of war were the ones that gave Moses a lot of problems because they represented the flesh. These men of war constantly waged war against Moses leadership and all it represented. The flesh against the Spirit (Galatians 5)

'And it came to pass, when they had done circumcising all the people, that they abode in their places in the camp, till they were whole. And the LORD said unto Joshua, This day have I rolled away the reproach of Egypt from off you. Wherefore the name of the place is called Gilgal unto this day. And the children of Israel encamped in Gilgal, and kept the Passover on the fourteenth day of the month at even in the plains of Jericho. And they did eat of the old corn of the land on the morrow after the Passover, unleavened cakes, and parched corn in the selfsame day. And the manna ceased on the morrow after they had eaten of the old corn of the land; neither had the children of Israel manna any more; but they did eat of the fruit of the land of Canaan that year.'

Joshua 5:8 - 12 (KJV)

From the above Scripture, we should examine and take note of some words like:

1. **Till they were made whole** - meaning that the process of circumcision was successfully completed. The flesh was subjected to the Spirit. They were no more carnal - so to say.

2. **Reproach of Egypt** - meaning that although they were freed from slavery in Egypt, but the mindset of slavery was still with them until it was removed from the Children of Israel at Gilgal through the mechanism of circumcision.

3. **Gilgal** - so the place was called Gilgal ('To End') unto this day, the place was named because of circumcision which took place there. God put an 'end' to their slavery mentality.

4. **Passover at Gilgal** - Passover is a feast that is symbolized with blood. It was simply the cleansing of the sinner with the blood of the Lamb. While the Children of Israel were still at Gilgal after their full circumcision, they observed the Passover - it was a double or complete blessing for them. The process of time (time to come into maturity) was completed while at Gilgal!

5. **Manna ceased** - Next day after the Passover, they ate from the gardens and grain fields which they invaded. The next day after (two days after Passover) no Manna fell, and IT WAS NEVER SEEN AGAIN!

Until we come to maturity by subjecting our flesh, we might not fully realized all the promises of God. In other words, what stands between you and the promises of God is not Satan, but sin. And until the flesh is dealt with, the issue of sins will continue to resurface.

Whenever Manna cease in your life journey, be happy for God has a better thing in stock for you. Rejoice when Manna cease.

Chapter Five

Destination

In many Christian gatherings, it is not likely for you not to hear the word Destiny. So, many things and lessons have been taught directly or indirectly on destiny as a topic. A lot of prayers have been offered on fulfilling your destiny, and many sermons preached on selfsame subject.

But of what use is a destiny with no destination? These two words are very important in anyone's life. Howbeit, if we can just calm down, I would love us to look up the definition of these words from the Dictionary

The event that may necessarily happen to a particular person in the future is *Destiny*.

The place to which someone is going or being sent is *Destination*.

In the year 2003, I was given a big job as a Director of an Organization, but the moment I resumed the office, I knew that it was not my calling. Although I gained some bureaucratic knowledge there, but my passion, my fire, my life was not put into the best use in the office - I am an Evangelist, a Kingdom teacher with a prophetic mandate, so sitting behind the computer everyday was not my calling, and I almost felt empty doing what was not part of my destiny.

Apostle Paul wrote to the Corinthians on somehow the same subject:

'But we have this treasure in earthen vessels, that the excellency of the power may be of God, and not of us.' - **2 Corinthians 4:7 (KJV)**

When you are on the right path of success, it is like a treasure inside of you. Every day brings its fulfillment to you and you are not easily burn out because you are on a divine mission.

Jesus had it thus:

'The Spirit of the Lord is upon me, because he hath anointed me to preach the gospel to the poor; he hath sent me to heal the brokenhearted, to preach deliverance to the captives, and recovering of sight to the blind, to set at liberty them that are bruised.'

- Luke 4:18 (KJV)

Jesus was born to be a King, and His Kingdom is not of this world, but it would be known through the above Mission Statement.

One of the greatest tragedies in life is people not reaching their destinations before they pass on to the great beyond. There are so many reasons responsible for this tragedy, chief among which is distraction - Not being focus on your goal in life.

Until you get to your destination and spelled out your destiny, life may not have real meaning to you. Time and Place are two major factors that enhance your destiny. Listen to this:

Job said he will wait for his appointed *time* which is from God (Job 14:14). God said to Ezekiel that He will place Israel into *their own land* (Ezekiel 37:14). These two factors are very sensitive ones when it comes to realizing your destiny that is why many people take it up to God for His leading.

People say life begins at forty, but I tell you the truth, life begins when you arrive your destination. This is the very place when you bring out with joy all the package of your destiny. Most times when we are traveling by road to Port - Harcourt from Ibadan, we continue the journey for about three hours, and then the Driver will pull over at Benin - Ore Road, and every passenger on board will get down to have something to eat and also to refresh themselves before they continue the eight hours journey. Benin - Ore Road is not their destination, so they will not bring out or unpack their bags and baggage.

The same is applicable in real life, there are so many destiny stop - overs, before the final destination. Many students of higher institutions pick up one or two odd jobs to support themselves financially before they graduate. Those jobs are destiny stop - over jobs, they are not the final destinations of these students, many of whom are destined to change the course of history!

Peter and Paul were two great apostles of our Lord Jesus Christ who had two different borders of destiny. Peter was sent basically to the Jews, while Paul was sent to the Gentiles. Each time these two crossed outside their border of destiny, they seem to have little problem directly or indirectly. Your border of destiny is the place God assigned for you to carry out your divine assignment, and bring glory to His Name.

You may travel all over the world, if your time has not come, people will not notice what you are doing around the world. Jesus told Mary His mother in John chapter two that His time has not come. The book of Ecclesiastes says there is time for everything under the heaven.

'To everything there is a season, and a time to every purpose under the heaven.' - **Ecclesiastes 3:1 (KJV)**

Waiting for their appointed time is one of the most difficult things learned by men of destiny. Seasons and Times are in the hands of God, man can only position himself and be ready.

'It is the glory of God to conceal a thing: but the honor of kings is to search out a matter.' - **Proverbs 25:2 (KJV)**

The full meaning of the above scripture will not be realized and appreciated until we check it out in other versions of the Bible.

There is a Word attached to your destiny right from birth, but you as a king must take time to search it out. God has chosen Jeremiah as a Prophet from the womb, and so was Paul the apostle chosen from birth to reveal the mystery of Christ - these are men of destiny who attested to what God called them to do even from birth!

'God conceals the revelation of his word in the hiding place of his glory. But the honor of kings is revealed by how they thoroughly search out the deeper meaning of all that God says.' - **Proverbs 25:2 (TPT)**

The 'Word' in the above version is what some versions called the 'matter', but the Hebrew 'dabar' is translated as the Word about eight hundred timed in the Old Testament. It is the revelation of this Word that your destiny wants to speaks about - but we need to search it out first as kings and priests.

Offence and *bad friends* can lead you away from your destination. These two factors, the Bible talks about in plain language. Jesus would not take offence at His accusers, the reason He prayed for them that Father should forgive them because they didn't know what they were doing. Stephen did the same thing to those that falsely accused and stoned him to death - he prayed for their forgiveness. Offence will make you to be offended which means going off - end your destination.

In teaching the keys of the Kingdom, offence is a major key that pulls people away from the Kingdom of God. Jesus said so many things about it in the Bible, and climaxed it with this; if you do not forgive, your heavenly Father will not forgive you too!

Ammon was one of king David's sons with a bright future and undeniable glorious destiny, but a bad friend ruined it all:

'But Amnon had a friend, whose name was Jonadab, the son of Shimeah David's brother: and Jonadab was a very subtil man. And he said unto him, why art thou, being the king's son, lean from day to day? Wilt thou not tell me? And Amnon said unto him, I love Tamar, my brother Absalom's sister. And Jonadab said unto him, Lay thee down on thy bed, and make thyself sick: and when thy father cometh to see thee, say unto him, I pray thee, let my sister Tamar come, and give me meat, and dress the meat in my sight, that I may see it, and eat it at her hand.'

- 2 Samuel 13:3 - 5 (KJV)

The evil scheme of a bad friend led Ammon to rape his step - sister which invariably resulted into Absalom's fury, and he killed Ammon - putting an end to Ammon's destiny without him reaching his destination in life.

Let's have a recap;

In reaching your destination with your packaged

destiny, there are two major factors which are:

1. God Factor:

a) Time: It is only God that determines the when a *process of time* becomes the *fullness of time* of a destiny. Howbeit, a man must wait patiently to complete his training from God and come to maturity in the fullness of time.

b) Place: God has set the borders of destiny for us all. It takes the leading of the Holy Spirit for us to follow as the Israel followed the Pillars in the wilderness. The wise men from the East were also led by the Star to the place where the Child was laid.

2. Man Factor:

a) Offence: Offence will surely come into a man's destiny, you cannot pray that out. No, you cannot. The purpose of offence is to throw you off - end your destination as you are offended. Primarily you forgive so that you can set yourself free from the self - imprisonment, and also to return back to your path of destiny which you have wandered away from due to anger and resentment.

b) Bad Friend: A bad friend is a destroyer of destiny that Satan has planted inside your inner circle of influence. Evil communications corrupt good manners. You may not choose your family, but you can choose your friend. Be not deceived, your friends can affect your destiny in any way possible.

Chapter Six

Speaking Destinies

AGNES GONXHA BOJAXHIU – MOTHER THERESA

Mother Teresa was born on 26 August, 1910 in Skopje, Macedonia. Mother Teresa's original name was Agnes Gonxha Bojaxhiu. The youngest of the children born to Nikola and Drane Bojaxhiu. Her father was a successful merchant and she was youngest of the three siblings. She received her First Communion at the age of five and a half and was confirmed in November 1916. From the day of her First Holy Communion, a love for souls was within her. Her father's sudden death when Gonxha was about eight years old left in the family in financial straits. Drane raised her children firmly and lovingly, greatly influencing her daughter's character and vocation. Gonxha's religious formation was further assisted by the vibrant Jesuit parish of the Sacred Heart in which she was much involved. At the age of twelve, she decided that she wanted to be a missionary and spread the love of Christ. At the age of eighteen she left her parental home in Skopje and joined the Sisters of Loreto, an Irish community of nuns with missions in India. There she received the name Sister Mary Teresa after St. Thérèse of Lisieux.

After a few months of training at the Institute of the Blessed Virgin Mary in Dublin Mother Teresa came to India on 6 January 1929. On 24 May, 1931, she took her initial vows as a nun. From 1931 to 1948, Mother Teresa taught geography and catechism at St. Mary's High School in Calcutta. On 24 May 1937, Sister Teresa made her Final Profession of Vows, becoming, as she said, the "spouse of Jesus" for "all eternity." From that time on she was called Mother Teresa. She continued teaching at St. Mary's and in 1944 became the school's principal. A person of profound prayer and deep love for her religious sisters and her students, Mother Teresa's twenty years in Loreto were filled with profound happiness. Noted for her charity, unselfishness and courage, her capacity for hard work and a natural talent for organization, she lived out her consecration to Jesus, in the midst of her companions, with fidelity and joy.

Mother Teresa's words are 'By blood, I am Albanian. By citizenship, an India. By faith, I am a Catholic Nun. As to my calling, I belong to the world. As to my heart, I belong entirely to the Heart of Jesus.'

RAVI ZACHARIAS

Although, at his death, there were some allegations against this man of destiny, yet I feel strongly to include his biography among those that God raised from grass to grace.

If we choose to learn from his errors, and look straight into his struggles in life, we can still hear his destiny speaks.

Ravi Zacharias is an Indian-born Canadian-American Christian apologist.

He is the founder and chairman of the board of Ravi Zacharias International Ministries, host of the radio programs *Let My People Think* and *Just Thinking*

A defender of evangelical Protestantism, Ravi is the author of numerous Christian books, including the Gold Medallion Book Award winner – *Can Man Live Without God?* in the category "theology and doctrine" and Christian bestsellers *Light in the Shadow of Jihad* and *The Grand Weaver*. He has had six honorary doctoral degrees, including a Doctor of Laws and a Doctor of Sacred Theology.

Evangelical Christian leader Chuck Colson referred to Zacharias as "the great apologist of our time."

Early Life

Born on 26 March 1946 in Madras, India, to a woman of the Nambudiri Brahmin caste and a Christian man of the Boatman caste. His mother was from Madras while his father was from Kerala. He grew up in Delhi.

According to Zacharias, before her marriage, Swiss German missionaries had spoken to his Brahmin ancestor about Christianity and she had converted and had been made an outcast by her Brahmin family and community.

Zacharias grew up in a nominal Anglican household, and says that he was an atheist until the age of seventeen when he tried to commit suicide by swallowing poison. While in the hospital, a local Christian worker brought him a Bible and told his mother to read to him from John 14. Zacharias says that it was John 14:19 that touched him and meant to him as the defining paradigm: "Because I live, you also will live." He said that he thought, "This may be my only hope: A new way of living. Life as defined by the Author of Life." and that he committed his life to Christ praying, "Jesus if You are the one who gives life as it is meant to be, I want it. Please get me out of this hospital bed well, and I promise I will leave no stone unturned in my pursuit of truth." In 1966 Zacharias emigrated with his family to Canada, earning his undergraduate degree from the Ontario Bible College in 1972 (now Tyndale University College & Seminary) and his M.Div. from Trinity International University.

Ministry

When former skeptic and seventeen-year-old Ravi Zacharias heard the words of Jesus in John 14:19, "Because I live, you also will live," the trajectory of his life changed forever. In a time of helplessness and unbelief—when he was on a bed of suicide—the truth of Scripture brought hope to Zacharias, and he committed his life to Christ, promising, "I will leave no stone unturned in my pursuit of truth." Earlier in John 14, Jesus says, "I am the way, and the truth, and the life." This verse has become the cornerstone of Zacharias's ultimate mission as a Christian apologist and evangelist: to present and defend the truth of Jesus Christ that others may find life in Him.

Zacharias's calling to preach was first confirmed when he was awarded the Asian Youth Preacher Award at the international Youth Congress in Hyderabad at the age of nineteen. Years later, the Billy Graham Evangelistic Association invited Zacharias to be a plenary speaker at the inaugural International Conference for Itinerant Evangelists ("Amsterdam '83") to address a gathering of four thousand other speakers. It would be another turning point for him, as he began to seriously consider the critical need of apologetics to remove the intellectual and existential barriers that kept many skeptics from considering the truth claims of Christ. A year later, in 1984, he founded Ravi Zacharias International Ministries (RZIM).

Ravi Zacharias is Founder and President of Ravi Zacharias International Ministries (RZIM), which celebrated its thirtieth anniversary in 2014. Dr. Zacharias has spoken all over the world for over forty-three years in scores of universities, notably Harvard, Dartmouth, Johns Hopkins, and Cambridge. He has addressed writers of the peace accord in South Africa and military officers at the Lenin Military Academy and the Center for Geopolitical Strategy in Moscow. At the invitation of the President of Nigeria, he addressed delegates at the First Annual Prayer Breakfast for African Leaders held in Mozambique.

Mr. Zacharias has direct contact with key leaders, senators, congressmen, and governors who consult him on an ongoing basis. He has addressed the Florida Legislature and the Governor's Prayer Breakfast in Texas and Louisiana, and has twice spoken at the Annual Prayer Breakfast at the United Nations in New York, which marks the beginning of the UN General Assembly each year. As the 2008 Honorary Chairman of the National Day of Prayer, he gave addresses at the White House, the Pentagon, and The Cannon House. He has had the privilege of addressing the National Prayer Breakfasts in the seats of government in Ottawa, Canada, and London, England, and speaking at the CIA in Washington, DC.

Zacharias was invited to spend the summer of 1971 in Vietnam, where he evangelized to the American soldiers, as well as to POWs and Viet Cong. After graduating from the Ontario Bible College, he began an itinerant ministry with the Christian and Missionary Alliance in Canada. In 1974 the C&MA sent him to Cambodia, where he preached only a short time before its fall to the Khmer Rouge. In 1977, after graduating from Trinity, Zacharias was commissioned to preach worldwide

In 1983, Zacharias was invited to speak in Amsterdam at the Billy Graham Evangelistic Association's annual evangelists' conference. It was here that he first noticed a lack of ministry in the area of Christian apologetics. After Amsterdam, Zacharias spent the summer evangelizing in India, where he continued to see the need for apologetics ministry, both to lead people to Christ and to train Christian leaders. In August 1984 Ravi Zacharias International Ministries was founded in Toronto, Canada to pursue his calling as a "classical evangelist in the arena of the intellectually resistant." Today its headquarters is located in Atlanta, Georgia, and has offices in Canada, India, Singapore, the United Kingdom, the Middle East, Hong Kong, Romania, Turkey, Austria, Spain, and South Africa. He was later ordained by the Christian and Missionary Alliance and commissioned as an international evangelist.

In 1989, shortly after the fall of the Berlin Wall, Zacharias was invited to speak in Moscow. While there he spoke to students at the Lenin Military Academy as well as political leaders at the Center for Geopolitical Strategy. This was the first of many evangelism opportunities toward the political world. Future events included an invitation to Bogota, Colombia in 1993, where he spoke to the judiciary committee on the importance of having a solid moral foundation.

AKINWUMI AKIN ADESINA

Dr. Akinwumi Akin Adesina was born on the 6 February, 1960 to a Nigerian farmer in Ibadan, Oyo State. He had his early education is a village school and proceeded to the University of Ife, Nigeria where he graduated with a Bachelors in Agricultural Economics with First Class Honors. He furthered his education at the Purdue University in Indiana and returned to Nigeria in 1984 to get married to Grace.

In 1988, he finally obtained his PhD (Agricultural Economics) and won the Outstanding PhD Thesis for his research work.

Career

In 1990, he stated serving as a senior economist at West African Rice Development Association (WARDA) in Bouaké, Ivory Coast. The appointment ended in 1995.

He also worked as the representative of the Rockefeller Foundation from 1999 to 2008. From 2003 until 2008 he served as an associate director for food security.

Dr. Akinwumi Adesina served as the Minister of Agriculture and Rural Development in Nigeria from 2010 to 2015. Due to his reform in the of Nigerian agriculture, he was named as Forbes African Man of the Year.

Among his good works was the introduction of more transparency into the fertilizer supply chain. He also planned giving out mobile phones to farmers though it proved difficult due to that lack of mobile network in some Nigerian areas. In 2010, Ban Ki-moon, the UN Secretary General appointed Akinwumi as one of the seventeen global leaders to spearhead the Millennium Development Goals. Akinwumi Adesina became the first Nigerian to hold the post of the President of the African Development Bank after he was elected on the 28 May, 2015. He launched a master plan based on energy, industrialization, agriculture, regional integration and bettering Africans' lives.

In 2016, he was again appointed by Ban Ki-moon to serve as member of the Lead Group of the Scaling Up Nutrition Movement.

Personal Life

Akinwumi Adesina met his wife while schooling at the Purdue University, Indiana, United States. They both worked with another couple and started a Christian group called the African Student Fellowship.

Akinwumi Adesina and Grace Adesina are happily married and have two children, Rotimi and Segun.

NICHOLAS JAMES VUJICIC

Nick Vujicic was born to Dushka and Boris Vujicic in 1982 in Melbourne, Australia. Although he was an otherwise healthy baby, Nick was born without arms and legs; he had no legs, but two small feet, one of which had two toes. Nick has two siblings, Michelle and Aaron. Initially, a Victoria state law prevented Nick from attending a mainstream school due to his physical disability in spite of a lack of mental impairment. However, Vujicic became one of the first physically disabled students integrated into a mainstream school once those laws changed. However, his lack of limbs made him a target for school bullies, and he fell into a severe depression. At age eight, he contemplated suicide and even tried to drown himself in his bathtub at age ten; his love for his parents prevented him from following through. He also stated in his music video "Something More" that God had a plan for his life and he could not bring himself to drown because of this.

Nick prayed very hard that God would give him arms and legs, and initially told God that, if his prayer remained unanswered, Nick would not praise him indefinitely. However, a key turning point in his faith came when his mother showed him a newspaper article about a man dealing with a severe disability. Vujicic realized he wasn't unique in his struggles and began to embrace his lack of limbs. After this, Nick realized his accomplishments could inspire others and became grateful for his life.

Nick gradually figured out how to live a full life without limbs, adapting many of the daily skills limbed people accomplish without thinking. Nick writes with two toes on his left foot and a special grip that slid onto his big toe. He knows how to use a computer and can type up to forty-five words per minute using the "heel and toe" method. He has also learned to throw tennis balls, play drum pedals, get a glass of water, comb his hair, brush his teeth, answer the phone and shave, in addition to participating in golf, swimming, and even sky-diving.

During secondary school, he was elected captain of MacGregor State in Queensland and worked with the student council on fundraising events for local charities and disability campaigns. When he was seventeen, he started to give talks at his prayer group, and later founded his non-profit organization, Life Without Limbs.

KENNETH HAGIN

Kenneth Erwin Hagin was an influential American Charismatic preacher born on 20 August, 1917 in McKinney, Texas to the family of Lillie Viola Drake Hagin and Jess Hagin. He was so small and lifeless that the doctor thought that he was stillborn.

Personal Life

He was married to Oretha Rooker. They had two children, a son, Kenneth Wayne Hagin, who is presently the pastor of Rhema Bible Church and President of Kenneth Hagin Ministries, and a daughter, Patricia Harrison. She is the widow of the late Doyle "Buddy' Harrison and is the owner and publisher of Harrison House, located in Tulsa, Oklahoma.

According to Hagin's testimony, he was sickly as a child, suffering from a deformed heart and what was believed to be an incurable blood disease. He became bedfast at age fifteen and was not expected to live. In April 1933 during a dramatic conversion experience, he reported dying three times in ten minutes, each time seeing the horrors of hell and then returning to life. But in August 1934, he was miraculously healed, raised off a deathbed by the power of God and the revelation of faith in God's Word. Jesus appeared to Rev. Hagin eight times over the next several years in visions that changed the course of his ministry.

Two years later he preached his first sermon as the pastor of a small community church in Roland, Texas, nine miles from McKinney.

In 1967, he began a regular radio broadcast that continues today as Rhema for Today.

His favorite scripture was Mark 11:23: "For verily I say unto you, That whosoever shall say unto this mountain, be thou removed and be thou cast into the sea, and shall not doubt in his heart, but shall believe that those things which he saith shall come to pass, he shall have whatsoever he saith."

Many of his followers often called him "Dad Hagin", "Papa Hagin", and more commonly "Brother Hagin". He is also often referred to as the "father" (or "granddaddy") of the "Word of Faith" movement. Hagin never received any formal theological training; however, he received an honorary doctorate from *Oral Roberts University* in the 1970s.

Papa-kenneth-hagin

Ministry

Hagin began an itinerant ministry as a Bible teacher and evangelist in 1949. He was also a part of the Voice of Healing Revival in the U.S. in the forties and fifties together with Oral Roberts, Gordon Lindsay and T. L. Osborn. In 1963, Kenneth E. Hagin Evangelistic Association was incorporated, and in 1966, the ministry offices moved to Tulsa, Oklahoma. That same year, he taught for the first time on radio — on KSKY in Dallas. In 1967, he began a regular radio broadcast that continues today as Faith Seminar of the Air. Teaching by his son, Rev. Kenneth Wayne Hagin, is also heard on the program.

Since its inception in 1963, his organization grew to include numerous media outreaches and ministries. These are:

• Faith Library Publications – with sixty-five million book copies in circulation

• "RHEMA Praise" – a weekly television program on the Trinity Broadcasting Network

• "Faith Seminar of the Air" – a radio program heard on many stations nationwide and on the Internet

- "The Word of Faith" – a free monthly magazine with roughly 600,000 subscribers
- crusades conducted throughout the nation
- RHEMA Correspondence Bible School
- the RHEMA Prayer and Healing Center, located on the Rhema campus in Broken Arrow, Oklahoma

RHEMA Bible Training College

Rhema Bible Training Centre

In 1974 Rev. Hagin founded what is now **Rhema Bible Training College** (RBTC). RBTC is an unaccredited Bible institute located on 110 acres (0.45 km^2) in Broken Arrow, a suburb of Tulsa, Oklahoma, USA. The curriculum is taught from a Charismatic/Pentecostal heritage. There are seven ministry concentrations specializing in Children's Ministry, Youth Ministry, Evangelism, Pastoral Care, Missions, Biblical Studies, and Supportive Ministry.

The school has campuses in many countries of the world including Austria, Brazil, Colombia, Germany, India, Indonesia, Italy, Mexico, Peru, Romania, Singapore, South Africa, the South Pacific, Thailand, Nigeria, Zambia, Egypt, and the Philippines.

Rhema-bible-training-college-celebrating-forty-years-of-graduates-1974-2014

RBTC also has over forty thousand graduates who reside and minister in more than hundred countries.

In 1979, he founded the Prayer and Healing Center there to provide a place for the sick to come to "have the opportunity to build their faith." Its Healing School continues to be held free of charge twice daily on the RHEMA campus.

After Kenneth E. Hagin's death in 2003, his son Kenneth W. Hagin continued to run the RBTC.

NELSON MANDELA

Rolihlahla Mandela was born into the Madiba clan in the village of Mvezo, in the Eastern Cape, on 18 July 1918. His mother was Nonqaphi Nosekeni and his father was Nkosi Mphakanyiswa Gadla Mandela, principal counsellor to the Acting King of the Thembu people, Jongintaba Dalindyebo.

In 1930, when he was twelve years old, his father died and the young Rolihlahla became a ward of Jongintaba at the Great Place in Mqhekezweni.

Hearing the elders' stories of his ancestors' valor during the wars of resistance, he dreamed also of making his own contribution to the freedom struggle of his people.

He attended primary school in Qunu where his teacher, Miss Mdingane, gave him the name Nelson, in accordance with the custom of giving all schoolchildren "Christian" names.

He completed his Junior Certificate at Clarkebury Boarding Institute and went on to Healdtown, a Wesleyan secondary school of some repute, where he matriculated.

Mandela began his studies for a Bachelor of Arts degree at the University College of Fort Hare but did not complete the degree there as he was expelled for joining in a student protest.

On his return to the Great Place at Mqhekezweni the King was furious and said if he didn't return to Fort Hare he would arrange wives for him and his cousin Justice. They ran away to Johannesburg instead, arriving there in 1941. There he worked as a mine security officer and after meeting Walter Sisulu, an estate agent, he was introduced to Lazer Sidelsky. He then did his articles through a firm of attorneys – Witkin, Eidelman and Sidelsky.

He completed his BA through the University of South Africa and went back to Fort Hare for his graduation in 1943.*n the steps of Wits University.(Image: ersity Archives)*

Meanwhile, he began studying for an LLB at the University of the Witwatersrand. By his own admission he was a poor student and left the university in 1952 without graduating. He only started studying again through the University of London after his imprisonment in 1962 but also did not complete that degree.

In 1989, while in the last months of his imprisonment, he obtained an LLB through the University of South Africa. He graduated in absentia at a ceremony in Cape Town.

Entering politics

Mandela, while increasingly politically involved from 1942, only joined the African National Congress in 1944 when he helped to form the ANC Youth League (ANCYL).

In 1944 he married Walter Sisulu's cousin, Evelyn Mase, a nurse. They had two sons, Madiba Thembekile "Thembi" and Makgatho, and two daughters both called Makaziwe, the first of whom died in infancy. He and his wife divorced in 1958.

Mandela rose through the ranks of the ANCYL and through its efforts, the ANC adopted a more radical mass-based policy, the Programme of Action, in 1949.

In 1952 he was chosen as the National Volunteer-in-Chief of the Defiance Campaign with Maulvi Cachalia as his deputy. This campaign of civil disobedience against six unjust laws was a joint programme between the ANC and the South African Indian Congress. He and 19 others were charged under the Suppression of Communism Act for their part in the campaign and sentenced to nine months of hard labor, suspended for two years.

A two-year diploma in law on top of his BA allowed Mandela to practice law, and in August 1952 he and Oliver Tambo established South Africa's first black-owned law firm in the 1950s, Mandela & Tambo.

At the end of 1952 he was banned for the first time. As a restricted person he was only permitted to watch in secret as the Freedom Charter was adopted in Kliptown on 26 June 1955.

The Treason Trial

Mandela was arrested in a countrywide police swoop on 5 December, 1956, which led to the 1956 Treason Trial. Men and women of all races found themselves in the dock in the marathon trial that only ended when the last 28 accused, including Mandela, were acquitted on 29 March, 1961.

On 21 March, 1960 police killed 69 unarmed people in a protest in Sharpeville against the pass laws. This led to the country's first state of emergency and the banning of the ANC and the Pan Africanist Congress (PAC) on 8 April. Mandela and his colleagues in the Treason Trial were among thousands detained during the state of emergency.

During the trial Mandela married a social worker,

Winnie Madikizela, on 14 June, 1958. They had two daughters, Zenani and Zindziswa. The couple divorced in 1996.

Days before the end of the Treason Trial, Mandela travelled to Pietermaritzburg to speak at the All-in Africa Conference, which resolved that he should write to Prime Minister Verwoerd requesting a national convention on a non-racial constitution, and to warn that should he not agree there would be a national strike against South Africa becoming a republic. After he and his colleagues were acquitted in the Treason Trial, Mandela went underground and began planning a national strike for 29, 30 and 31 March.

In the face of massive mobilization of state security the strike was called off early. In June 1961 he was asked to lead the armed struggle and helped to establish Umkhonto weSizwe (Spear of the Nation), which launched on 16 December 1961 with a series of explosions.

Madiba travelled with his Ethiopian passport.
(Image: © National Archives of South Africa)

On 11 January, 1962 using the adopted name David Motsamayi, Mandela secretly left South Africa. He travelled around Africa and visited England to gain support for the armed struggle. He received military training in Morocco and Ethiopia and returned to South Africa in July 1962. He was arrested in a police roadblock outside Howick on 5 August while returning from KwaZulu-Natal, where he had briefed ANC President Chief Albert Luthuli about his trip.

He was charged with leaving the country without a

permit and inciting workers to strike. He was convicted and sentenced to five years' imprisonment, which he began serving at the Pretoria Local Prison. On 27 May, 1963 he was transferred to Robben Island and returned to Pretoria on 12 June. Within a month police raided Liliesleaf, a secret hideout in Rivonia, Johannesburg, used by ANC and Communist Party activists, and several of his comrades were arrested.

On 9 October 1963 Mandela joined 10 others on trial for sabotage in what became known as the Rivonia Trial. While facing the death penalty his words to the court at the end of his famous "Speech from the Dock" on 20 April 1964 became immortalized:

"I have fought against white domination, and I have fought against black domination. I have cherished the ideal of a democratic and free society in which all persons live together in harmony and with equal opportunities. It is an ideal which I hope to live for and to achieve. But if needs be, it is an ideal for which I am prepared to die."

Speech from the Dock quote by Nelson Mandela on 20 April 1964

On 11 June, 1964 Mandela and seven other accused, Walter Sisulu, Ahmed Kathrada, Govan Mbeki, Raymond Mhlaba, Denis Goldberg, Elias Motsoaledi and Andrew Mlangeni, were convicted and the next day were sentenced to life imprisonment. Goldberg was sent to Pretoria Prison because he was white, while the others went to Robben Island.

Mandela's mother died in 1968 and his eldest son, Thembi, in 1969. He was not allowed to attend their funerals.

On 31 March, 1982 Mandela was transferred to Pollsmoor Prison in Cape Town with Sisulu, Mhlaba and Mlangeni. Kathrada joined them in October. When he returned to the prison in November 1985 after prostate surgery, Mandela was held alone. Justice Minister Kobie Coetsee visited him in hospital. Later Mandela initiated talks about an ultimate meeting between the apartheid government and the ANC.

mage: © National Archives of South Africa)
Release from prison
On 12 August, 1988 he was taken to hospital where he was diagnosed with tuberculosis. After more than three months in two hospitals he was transferred on 7 December, 1988 to a house at Victor Verster Prison near Paarl where he spent his last 14 months of imprisonment. He was released from its gates on Sunday 11 February, 1990, nine days after the unbanning of the ANC and the PAC and nearly four months after the release of his remaining Rivonia comrades. Throughout his imprisonment he had rejected at least three conditional offers of release.

Mandela immersed himself in official talks to end white minority rule and in 1991 was elected ANC President to replace his ailing friend, Oliver Tambo. In 1993 he and President FW de Klerk jointly won the Nobel Peace Prize and on 27 April, 1994 he voted for the first time in his life.

President
On 10 May, 1994 he was inaugurated as South Africa's first democratically elected President. On his 80th birthday in 1998 he married Graça Machel, his third wife.

True to his promise, Mandela stepped down in 1999 after one term as President. He continued to work with the Nelson Mandela Children's Fund he set up in 1995 and established the Nelson Mandela Foundation and The Mandela Rhodes Foundation.

"It is in your hands" – Mandela Day quote
174094413

In April 2007 his grandson, Mandla Mandela, was installed as head of the Mvezo Traditional Council at a ceremony at the Mvezo Great Place.

Nelson Mandela never wavered in his devotion to democracy, equality and learning. Despite terrible provocation, he never answered racism with racism. His life is an inspiration to all who are oppressed and deprived; and to all who are opposed to oppression and deprivation.

He died at his home in Johannesburg on 5 December 2013.

Live out your conviction – it is your destiny!

Chapter Seven

Speak, Don't Talk!

Action speaks louder than voice. What you do may outlive what you say in life. When a man matures, he speaks more and he talks less.
'In the multitude of words there wanteth not sin: but he that refraineth his lips is wise.' – **Proverbs 10:19 (KJV)**
Talk is cheap, talk is voluminous, but to make a small speech requires deep thinking. Winston S. Churchill once said that a good speech should be like a woman's skirt; long enough to cover the subject and short enough to create interest. To drive home my point, let me give you this picture: A man asked his friend if the guest speaker is done, the friend replied that the guest speaker has finished his speech, but he is still talking!

While talking involves conversation within two or more people, speaking in most cases focuses on the one that makes the sound/speech. Speaking is derived from speech which could be informative or instructive.

The Bible is always clear on the issue of talk and speech; it was never a mistake when you see these two words used in the Bible, especially when God was asking Moses to speak and to talk to the house of Jacob, and to the children of Israel. Jacob was a man that was not yet reformed, but Israel was Jacob reformed. Double identity of the same man!

In the same light, Abram gave birth to Ishmael, but Abraham fathered the promised son – Isaac! Abraham was NOT the father of Ishmael, it was unreformed Abram that gave birth to Ishmael. Many years later, the reformed Abraham fathered Isaac – for at his death, Abraham gave his other sons gifts, but the inheritance and the lineage was transferred to Isaac!

A destiny that speaks needs not be birth with a golden spoon, it is a destiny that has seen it all, and have learnt like Paul, how to abase and abound.

The destiny of Jacob was penned like this in the Bible:

'These are the generations of Jacob. Joseph, being seventeen years old, was feeding the flock with his brethren;' – **Genesis 37:2 (KJV)**

The Bible says these are the generations of Jacob (full stop), then it brought in Joseph, and continued with Joseph's story by a comma sign. It means that Jacob was the tree that produced Joseph the fruit, and by this fruit the entire generations of Jacob were preserved. So, the destiny of Jacob was written in the life of Joseph!

Amazingly, when the fruit was ripe enough, the tree took the glory at the zenith of his life. We must bear in mind that the Egypt of those days was the like America of these days. See how the Bible put it:

'And Joseph brought in Jacob his father, and set him before Pharaoh: and Jacob blessed Pharaoh. And Pharaoh said unto Jacob, How old art thou? And Jacob said unto Pharaoh, The days of the years of my pilgrimage are an hundred and thirty years: few and evil

have the days of the years of my life been, and have not attained unto the days of the years of the life of my fathers in the days of their pilgrimage. And Jacob blessed Pharaoh, and went out from before Pharaoh.'
 – **Genesis 47:7 – 10 (KJV)**

Twice from the above scripture, the Bible says AND JACOB BLESSED PHARAOH! Why would the king of a rich and civilized country bowed before a man of destiny to bless him? Simply because the fruit (has already dazzled the king with his finesse of wisdom and grace of God, so Pharaoh was looking forward to meet the tree that produced this excellent fruit – and when the king saw Jacob, he allowed Jacob to place a blessing upon him. Jacob's destiny spoke to Pharaoh. And when it was time for Jacob to talk with Pharaoh, Jacob talked less, because his destiny had already spoken!

Most boastful people are talkative; they are the ones with talking lips having little or no lesson to learn or dash out.

'Should not the multitude of words be answered? And should a man full of talk be justified?' – **Job 11:2 (KJV)**

When a man is identified with multitude of words, then he is likely to be a talkative.

'Talk no more so exceeding proudly; let not arrogancy come out of your mouth: for the LORD is a God of knowledge, and by him actions are weighed.' – **1 Samuel 2:3 (KJV)**

When we were children, we talked like children; we were so much excited that we were talking. However, as we age in life, we became mature with life, so we speak more and talk less – we are experienced!

'The Lord GOD hath given me the tongue of the

learned, that I should know how to speak a word in season to him that is weary: he wakeneth morning by morning, he wakeneth mine ear to hear as the learned.'
   - Isaiah 50:4(KJV)

When God gives you the tongue of the learned, you don't talk with such a tongue, you speak!

In South America and some other countries of the same clime, the aged with wisdom speaks, while the youth that needs advice and counseling talks. Their wisdom on many subjects of life are engraved and written in the marble of time.

You will need to talk a lot to convince people of your anointing, for example, but when your anointing speaks, people are instantly convinced that God called you. Ministers of letters are out there talking psychology to their congregations.

'Don't let anyone capture you with empty philosophies and high – sounding nonsense that come from human thinking and from the spiritual powers of this world, rather than from Christ.'
   – Colossians 2:8(NLT)

This same Apostle warned the congregation at Corinth about cheap talk:

'And my speech and my preaching were not with enticing words of man's wisdom, but in demonstration of the Spirit and of power.'
   - 1Corinthians 2:4 (KJV)

From the above verse, we know Apostle Paul was not talking, because he said 'and my speech' – a demonstration of the Spirit and of power.

The integrity of Apostle Paul's life was displayed in his letter to the Romans, where he amplified 'speech/speak', again – the summary of what his life reflects. Hear him:

'For I will not dare to speak of any of those things which Christ hath not wrought by me, to make the Gentiles obedient, by word and deed, Through mighty signs and wonders, by the power of the Spirit of God; so that from Jerusalem, and round about unto Illyricum, I have fully preached the gospel of Christ.' – **Romans 15:18/19 (KJV)**

Your destiny will speak through the things you have done or accomplished in life, but your tongue will talk to convince people of what you have in mind to do – your intentions in life.

'For we dare not make ourselves of the number, or compare ourselves with some that commend themselves: but they measuring themselves by themselves, and comparing themselves among themselves, are not wise.' **– 2 Corinthians 10:12 (KJV)**

Instead for the people Paul was referring to in above Scripture to work for the Lord God, they go about boasting (talking) within their circle of influence, and they commend themselves among themselves. The aged Apostles said these people were not wise. True to the Apostle Paul's word, we never see the record of these boastful people in any page of the Bible!

It is your habit that speaks through your destiny, and people pay attention to it. The Bible explains this further and better with the example of Abel;

'By faith Abel offered unto God a more excellent sacrifice than Cain, by which he obtained witness that he was righteous, God testifying of his gifts: and by it he being dead yet speaketh' – **Hebrews 11:4 (KJV)**

Can you see my point? ...And by it he being dead yet speaks! The summary of Abel's life is in honoring God with excellent sacrifice – his habit!

What we do every day with passion eventually forms our habits, and habits are cornerstone of our destinies. Even when you are not talking, your destiny is speaking! We cannot take prayer out of the life of Jesus Christ, our Lord and Savior. All the gospel writers testified to this truth in their writings, Luke 22:39 put it this way:

'And He came out and went, as was His habit, to the Mount of Olives; and the disciples followed Him,' – **(Amplified)**

Prayer became Jesus' habit to the very extent that when He was nailed to the Cross, despite the excruciating pains of the nails on His hands, He was still praying! One of the major virtues we learnt from Jesus' life and ministry is PRAYER

In another dimension, we see another habit of our Lord Jesus Christ, as given to us by the aged Apostle Peter:

'How God anointed Jesus of Nazareth with the Holy Ghost and with power: who went about doing good, and healing all that were oppressed of the devil; for God was with him.' – **Acts 10:38 (KJV)**

In addition to the habit of prayer, here we see the habit of DOING GOOD – Who went about (everywhere He goes) doing good!

In our lives, purpose is the most important aspect of our living. It is the answer to the why of life? To some extent, purpose can relate well with vision, only that it is clearer and readily received by all.

Where and when a purpose is lost, abuse became

inevitable! Another tragedy of mankind, especially the youth who has lost constraint to their vision, and ended up abusing their own destiny.

We will go back again to our Lord and Savior Jesus Christ, as our model for this same subject. Jesus' vision statement – the beginning to the ending of his vision was written in the book of (His destiny (we must find our destinies from God through His Word, the Bible) Isaiah. Jesus opened the book, read His own vision, and closed the book.

*'And when he had **opened the book**, he found the place where it was written, The Spirit of the Lord is upon me, because he hath anointed me to preach the gospel to the poor; he hath sent me to heal the brokenhearted, to preach deliverance to the captives, and recovering of sight to the blind, to set at liberty them that are bruised, To preach the acceptable year of the Lord. And he **closed the book**.'*
    - Luke 4:17 – 20 (KJV)(emphasis mine)

However, the summarized purpose of God sending Jesus to this world was clearly stated by the beloved Apostle John. Hear John:

'... For this purpose the Son of God was manifested, that he might destroy the works of the devil.' **– 1 John 3:8 (KJV)**

Jesus' purpose in coming to the world is to DESTROY THE WORKS OF THE DEVIL in many areas, ranging from Salvation to healing, deliverance, reconciliation, worship, etc.

Chapter Eight

Destiny Fulfilled in Jesus

'The eyes of your understanding being enlightened; that ye may know what is the hope of his calling, and what the riches of the glory of his inheritance in the saints,' – **Ephesians 1:18 (KJV)**

God created everyone for His particular purpose on earth. There is no one that is purposelessly living on earth today, although it is another thing if one has not realized the very purpose of his or her existing.

However, for Christians, the purpose of God is already revealed in Jesus Christ, who came to show us the will of God the Father. Christians find fulfillment of purpose only in the Will of God. Until when we come to maturity in our Christianity, we cannot confidently say THY WILL BE DONE.

With the view of making it in front of us, we all engaged in the rat race and forget the purpose of God for us as individuals. It is only when we get tired and exhausted in our race that we remember God and turn to Him for help – in a race that He did not send us to run.

We will find fulfillment and happiness in life if only we can do the will of God for us, especially as Christians.

A billionaire in a telephone interview was asked by the radio presenter, 'Sir what can you remember made you a happy man in life?

The billionaire said, 'I have gone through four stages of happiness in life and finally I understood the meaning of true happiness.

The first stage was to accumulate wealth and means. But at this stage I did not get the happiness I wanted.

Then came the second stage of collecting valuables and items. But I realized that the effect of this thing is also temporary and luster of valuable things does not last long.

Then came the third stage of getting big projects. That was when I was holding ninety five percent of diesel supply in Nigeria and Africa. I was also the largest vessel owner in Africa and Asia. But even here I did not get the happiness I had imagined.

The fourth stage was the time a friend of mine asked to buy wheelchair for some disabled children. Just about two hundred kids.

At the friend's request, I immediately bought the wheelchairs. But the friend insisted that I go with him and hand over the wheelchairs to the children. I got ready and went with him.

There I gave these wheelchairs to these children with my own hands. I saw the strange glow of happiness on the faces of these children. I saw them all sitting on the wheelchairs, moving around and having fun. It was as if they had arrived at a picnic spot where they are sharing a jackpot winning.

I felt real joy inside me. When I decided to leave, one of the kids grabbed my legs. I tried to free my legs gently but the child starred at my face and held my legs tightly.

I bent down and asked the child; do you need

something else? The answer this child gave me not only made me happy, but also changed my attitude to life completely. The child said, 'I want to remember your face so that when I meet you in heaven, I will be able to recognize you and thank you once again.'

In whatever we do, our fulfillment comes from making someone else happy, and giving God the glory. If these two conditions are not met, we are not yet fulfilled.

For the three Hebrew boys, the whole country was happy, and God took all the glory. Take a look at the story:

'Then Nebuchadnezzar came near to the mouth of the burning fiery furnace, and spake, and said, Shadrach, Meshach, and Abednego, ye servants of the most high God, come forth, and come hither. Then Shadrach, Meshach, and Abednego, came forth of the midst of the fire. And the princes, governors, and captains, and the king's counsellors, being gathered together, saw these men, upon whose bodies the fire had no power, nor was a hair of their head singed, neither were their coats changed, nor the smell of fire had passed on them.

Then Nebuchadnezzar spake, and said, blessed be the God of Shadrach, Meshach, and Abednego, who hath sent his angel, and delivered his servants that trusted in him, and have changed the king's word, and yielded their bodies, that they might not serve nor worship any god, except their own God. Therefore I make a decree, That every people, nation, and language, which speak anything amiss against the God of Shadrach, Meshach, and Abednego, shall be cut in pieces, and their houses shall be made a dunghill: because there is no other God that can deliver after this sort.' – **Daniel 3:26 – 29 (KJV)**

The whole country was happy because the citizens have the opportunity to know the true God, and Jehovah God was glorified throughout the regions. The king himself made the proclamation and evangelized the good news about knowing the true God.

Peter was introduced to us as a frustrated fisherman, but the day he had an encounter with Jesus, his destiny changed from grass to grace. This is how the Bible put it:

'When Simon Peter saw it, he fell down at Jesus' knees, saying, depart from me; for I am a sinful man, O Lord. For he was astonished, and all that were with him, at the draught of the fishes which they had taken: And so was also James, and John, the sons of Zebedee, which were partners with Simon. And Jesus said unto Simon, Fear not; from henceforth thou shalt catch men.' - **Luke 5:8 – 10 (KJV)**

Peter's destiny IN Jesus Christ was to catch men for the Kingdom of God! By the time Peter fully keyed into this great destiny of his in Christ Jesus, this same Peter preached a single sermon, and about three thousand souls gave their lives to Jesus genuinely! It got to a time that the shadow of Peter was healing the sick! The reed that was once tossed about by water eventually became a piece of the Rock that cannot be shaken!

Saul was a young and vibrant Jewish man who deeply hated the Way in his days. After he had obtained a letter of authority from the council of elders to persecute the Church, on his ways to Damascus, his destiny changed. Like Peter the fisherman, Saul also had an encounter with Jesus Christ. Read:

'And as he journeyed, he came near Damascus: and suddenly there shined round about him a light from heaven: And he fell to the earth, and heard a voice saying unto him, Saul, Saul, why persecutest thou me? And he said, Who art thou, Lord? And the Lord said, I am Jesus whom thou persecutest: it is hard for thee to kick against the pricks. And he trembling and astonished said, Lord, what wilt thou have me to do? And the Lord said unto him, Arise, and go into the city, and it shall be told thee what thou must do. And the men which journeyed with him stood speechless, hearing a voice, but seeing no man.'

– Acts 9:3 – 7 (KJV)

God later performed extra ordinary miracles through this man called Saul, who was also known as Paul, to the extent that aprons and handkerchiefs from his body were used in far places for deliverances!

Paul's destiny in Jesus Christ is still speaking till today, the destiny of a man who wrote more than half of the New Testament in the Bible!

Smith Wigglesworth was a plumber like any other plumber in his days, he could not accomplished much, no matter how hard he tried, until he found Christ Jesus. Smith's destiny in Christ, like Apostle Peter, was not to repair broken water pipes, but to link people to the Fountain of life which is Jesus Christ!

Ayo Babalola was working with a road construction company with nothing to show for it, until God called unto him like Saul, asking him to prepare for a great divine assignment. Babalola's complete obedience and dogged faith in God aligned his destiny into Christ Jesus, and an unprecedented history was made. Many of this

Apostle's unusual records are still with the Christ Apostolic Church (C.A.C) till this very day.

Jesus Christ is already great to the extent that at the mention of His Name – demons bow! If you therefore join Jesus to carry out what He (Jesus) has for you as an individual, you will be great! The baby elephant do not struggle or eat much to be big – it is hereditary, so is greatness with whoever aligned his or her destiny into Jesus Christ!

Millions of Christians all over the world, who are not necessary preachers or pastors, have outstanding testimonies of how their destinies were aligned into Christ Jesus, and they became great in their respective professions. Christopher Kolade is not a Pastor or a Preacher, but his success in life comes from his walk with Jesus Christ and his destiny in the hands of his Maker – God! Every one that has worked with this elder statesman confessed that he is a true Christian, successful in every areas of life with his destiny speaking.

Conclusion

'Abide in me, and I in you. As the branch cannot bear fruit of itself, except it abide in the vine; no more can ye, except ye abide in me.

I am the vine, ye are the branches: He that abideth in me, and I in him, the same bringeth forth much fruit: for without me ye can do nothing.'
John 15:4/5(KJV)

In a simple logic, how can you achieve anything in life without Jesus, after you have given your life to Jesus, as your personal Lord and Savior? From the above Scripture, where Jesus was talking to his disciples alone, He said to them (not to everybody), 'for without me you can do nothing.' Jesus has the destiny of every Christian in His hand, which is why He asked us to take up our cross and follow Him.

Until you come to the place of revelation, you will never know how wonderful and how glorious your destiny is in Christ Jesus. Allow me to give you an illustration – when John saw Babylon the great harlot with gold jewelries all over her body, John would have said to himself, what a wealth! But when John was asked to come up higher, and he saw the New Jerusalem with streets of Gold, John was perplexed and speechless! So is your destiny when you held on to it and copied the world, compared to when you handed it over to Jesus Christ.

These are some of the things that the world will packaged and presented to you in exchange for your destiny. On the other side, and opposite, are the things that Jesus will transfer to you once you placed you destiny in Christ:

WORLD	JESUS CHRIST
Happiness	Joy
Glamour	Glory
Popularity	Power
Money	Wealth
Medications	Long Life
Talent (puff up self)	Gift (glorify God)
Society Marriage	Lasting Home

Finally, let it be known to you that although your destiny is chosen by God, its fulfillment is decided by you. This is why I keep saying that Jesus Christ came to show us how to fully obey God to the letters.

It is in our total obedience that will locate and enter into the rest God has prepared for us – Our Destination, where our destinies are revealed and made known!

'There remaineth therefore a rest to the people of God. For he that is entered into his rest, he also hath ceased from his own works, as God did from his.' – **Hebrews 4:9/10 (KJV)**

Coming to the rest of God is all you ever need to do in your entire life. It does not mean sleeping or lying on your king size bed, but finally arriving your life destination, unpacking the bags and baggage of your life, living out your passion, being fulfilled every day!

No matter your age or your circumstances, ***there***

remaineth a rest to the people of God – simply means God is not quitting on you, you still have another opportunity with God, to enter His rest made, designed and arranged for you! It is not over yet – the implication of the word **REMAINS** in the above Scripture (Hebrews 4:9).

When your destiny begins to speak, it will not be boastful or haughty, but it will speak loud and clear of the LOVE of God, amplify the GRACE of our Lord Jesus Christ, and make known to others how sweet the FELLOWSHIP of the Holy Spirit is!

Friends, kindly permit me to summarize the substance of this wonderful book with this Hymn (composed in 1872) by Annie Sherwood Hawks, paying rapt attention to every word therein:

> *I need Thee every hour,*
> *Most gracious Lord,*
> *No tender voice like Thine,*
> *Can peace afford.*
> *I need Thee, O I need Thee,*
> *Every hour I need Thee!*
> *O bless me now, Savior,*
> *I come to Thee.*
> *I need Thee every hour,*
> *Stay Thou nearby,*
> *Temptations lose their pow'r*
> *When Thou art nigh*
>
> *I need Thee every hour,*

In joy or pain
Come quickly and abide,
Or life is vain.
I need Thee every hour,
Teach me Thy will,
And Thy rich promises
In me fulfill
I need Thee every hour,
Most Holy One,
O make me Thine indeed,
Thou blessed Son

Other Books by the Author

The Working Of His Mighty Power
Remedies (Biblical solutions to emotional illnesses)
Buy The Truth
The spirit of Nimrod
Strong meat, sharp teeth
Destroy this temple
Paradox of His Kingdom
Against All Odds
The Winning Wife published 11.15.2019 (LULU Publishers US) ISBN: 978-1-6847-1375-2